About The Author

I am a sales trainer and coach with a g[r]
growing businesses, managing, motiva[...]g and training
sales teams. My passion is sharing how you can grow your
business and find financial freedom through sales. Sales
has provided me the ultimate pathway to financial
freedom, which allows me to travel, spend time with family
or friends all while building and developing my own
business.

I was first interested in business and sales when I was very
young. In my childhood, I used to play tycoon video games
such as simtower, simcity, transport tycoon, and other
tycoon/enterprise games which might have been the
reason for my sales and business career that I chose later
in my life.

I never really knew what I wanted to do in high school or
even after I finished university. I didn't have high grades, I could not really focus on high school much.
Some probably could have said I had ADHD or something, but nevertheless, I graduated high school
and went to university. I did not have any idea of what I wanted to do but one thing was clear in my
mind; I wanted to make money and start a business. Hence, I completed a business degree with
majors in Accounting.

After graduating from University, I first went into working as a Tax Accountant, then to a multinational
conglomerate Toll Transport as a Management Accountant. Around 23 years of age, I quickly realised
there were far better paths to take than one tha involved staring at a spreadsheet for forty+ hours a
week. I wanted a career that allowed me to communicate and help people and I was sick of waking
up every morning, dreading the daily commute. I found the job boring and lifeless and I quit
eventually.

You may have said that that decision was wrong. I started drinking a lot and I found myself just
floating around not doing much. I knew I wanted to go somewhere but I just couldn't figure it out.

After that, I went into a sales job at Telstra telemarketing. This job changed my life forever. I started
controlling my life and It was here that I learnt the art of sale. My salary went from 50k to $100k at
Telstra eventually. But something was still missing, I wanted to enter the business development
lifestyle. Hence, I left this job in hopes of entering business development life.

I experienced a brief moment of despair and found myself living day to day again. But it was at this
juncture, that I realized I had to do what I want to do this time. I started my career in managing,
training, and coaching within my industry. I kicked my commitment into gear, and began teaching
myself everything there was to learn about sales. In a short time, I managed to turn around $1 million
in sales for a solar company.

Changing my career into sales was the best thing I ever did. I soon learnt life's most valuable lesson,
which is to get paid on what you produce and your effort. Sales teaches you to control your own
income based on the amount of effort you put in. How to grow the income of any business, and
generate multiple revenue streams.

Now, I want to give back what I have learned and help others achieve their goals in business and in
sales. I want everyone to know that you don't have to be really smart to be rich as you may have been
raised to believe. This is what gives me motivation to be here everyday. I realized my childhood
dream and now I want others to realize their dreams as well.

Jeremy Pearce
Outside Sales Training

Introduction

Sales is a people-business and to excel at sales, you have to learn how to deal with people on a daily basis. This book is a guide to all the great salesmen of the future. If you want to improve your sales skills, this is a great place to start. The book describes various proven sales techniques that you can use in your business as well as in your day to day life to achieve success and reach your goals.

The book is designed in a reader-friendly and a professional tone which helps greatly in understanding the complex sales terms, methods, strategies, and techniques. This book contains all the information you will ever need, from the fundamentals of sales, to the core skills and techniques you need to excel at sales and become a great salesman.

Most of us get tired from our day-to-day jobs and the attached salaries. Almost everyone wants to get rich and follow their dream life in one way or another. If you wake up one day and realize that you don't have to live your life on salaries and working for someone else, this book will be there to help you guide through a career in sales.

This book is divided into 14 Core chapters, with each chapter dealing with a specific sales process. The content of the chapters are authentic and have been taken from credible and respected sources. All the data and information contained in this book are up-to-date and state of the art techniques and skill sets are discussed.

The First chapter deals with the fundamentals of the sales process. It describes what sales basically is, and what you need to know about sales. One of the best things about the first chapter is that it describes the role of commissions. Commissions are one of the best things in business. The Second Chapter describes the Importance of Sales. Sales are the vital minute processes that drive the entire economies of the world.

The Third Chapter deals with the Reporting methods which are necessary for excelling at sales. This chapter describes the three main methods of tracking sales success, which are Accounting, CRM, and KPI. The Fourth Chapter lists three principles that you have to adopt in order to excel at sales. These are Commitment, Prediction, and Confidence.

Fifth Chapter deals with the science behind persuading others. This is one of the most important chapters of the book. It lists 6 shortcuts to persuade and influence someone. The sixth chapter focuses on goals, visions, and missions. Great companies and organizations work to solve problems and have a noble vision in mind for which they work day and night.
The Seventh and Eighth chapters focus on the importance of positivity and the need to focus on your own skills and not blame customers for sales drawbacks.These chapters are a great tool to help you guide through tough times and make you learn what you might be doing wrong in sales. Chapter 9 describes the "why" which is an important component of a company's existence.

The Final 5 chapters are the most important chapters of this book. They provide a complete guide for you to excel at sales. They will help you build your step by step sales process and discuss the rules of engagement in sales. One of the important aspects of sales is phone sales which is increasingly becoming important in this digital age. The last chapter deals with the metrics to measure your sales success.

Table of Contents

4 Three Principles of Excellency; Commitment, Prediction & Confidence

5 The Science Of Persuasion

6 The Pitch: Your "WHY"

11 Build Your Step by Step Sales Process

12 Sales And Marketing Metrics

BONUS CHAPTER
How to Excel at Phone Sales

CHAPTER 1

INTRODUCTION TO SALES

What Exactly is Sales and Selling?

American Society for Training and Development (ASTD) defines selling as,

"The holistic business system required to effectively develop, manage, enable, and execute a mutually beneficial, interpersonal exchange of goods or services for equitable value." (1)

The Wikipedia Dictionary Definition of selling is.

"The action of persuading a person or organization in expressing an interest in acquiring the offered item of value."
An organization or a person expressing an interest in acquiring the offered item of value is called a potential buyer, prospective customer, or prospect. It is said that buying and selling are the two sides of the same "coin" or transaction. Both the seller and the buyer engage in the process of negotiation for the exchange of any value. The exchange of value or the selling   process has defined rules and identifiable   stages. The selling process must proceed fairly and ethically so that both the parties involved

are equally rewarded. The different stages of selling and buying involve; getting acquainted, assessing each party's need for the other's item of value, and determining whether the values to be exchanged are equivalent or nearly so, or, in buyer's terms, "worth the price." Most frequently, sellers have to use their own experiences when selling products with appropriate discounts. (2) (Wikipedia)

The process of sales is a systematic process of repetitive and measurable milestones. The definition of selling is considered somewhat ambiguous. This is due to the close nature of advertising, public relations, promotion, and direct marketing. Selling is a profession-wide term like marketing. Almost everyone is considered a salesperson because we all have to sell something in life, whether it is a product, a service, or our abilities. However, efforts to understand who is or not a salesperson have established a separate profession for salespeople.

Selling is dependent on the human agents involved in the exchange between buyers and sellers. These agents are called salespeople or salespersons. They possess a specific set of sales skills and have the extensive knowledge required to facilitate the exchange of value between buyer and seller.

What is Sales all about?

What is sales all about? Well, Sales is a lifestyle, it's a career, it's a business. Sales truly make the world go round. Without sales, all businesses and industries would collapse. Sales is what keeps all types of exchanges in line; without it, we would not have been able to form civilization. The basis for civilization was the exchange of services and goods which is not possible without sales.

Selling is not a job or a career. It is a committed way of life. Selling is your natural skill to do well, survive, and prosper to create your financial position in life. It depends solely on your ability to sell on those things in which you believe. We are not talking about selling products or services here; We are talking about you selling yourself!

You either learn to negotiate, or someone else will negotiate the outcome. Want to buy a house one day? Want to sell a house one day? Getting a job? For each and every scenario in life, you have to learn how to negotiate. Negotiating is not just about products; you need to learn how to get others to agree to your demands. One must learn how to get another person's agreement to go to a restaurant at some point in life.

Selling is your ability to get others to like you. To be a true master at selling, you need to be able to get others to work with/for you. It is your ability to get others to support you. Selling is your ability to get people to want to please you, and make you feel good, and do things for you.

Starting one's own business is selling. Putting a business plan together to sell the bank on some financing for funding, what would you call that? That is selling!

Going to get a list for the property? Well, all that is convincing someone to do something and persuading others to support your ideas. That is Selling

Selling is, again, an act of persuading others. It is about convincing others to do something that you want them to do. It involves convincing, persuading, debating, and basically getting your way. Selling can be as simple as getting a friend to get a glass of water for you, and it can be as complex as getting multinational corporations to agree to the business idea you have in your mind.

Selling is an obligation to gain all the success you are ever going to create in life, no matter what you do, because selling has an impact on every person on this planet. Your Skills, or lack thereof, of selling, persuading, negotiating, and convincing others impacts every single area of life. Additionally, it determines how well you do in life, no matter your title or your position.

No matter where you are in life, no matter your role in the company or the team. It does not matter whether you are a janitor or a CEO. At some point, you will have to convince others of your position. What I mean by that is what you believe you can sell!. That belief, that idea, that concept you need to sell to someone else. Your skill to do so impacts you in ways that will determine the very fabric of your future. Selling is a part of every person, every day, all day around the world.

The sales process is all about reading the situations and knowing everything about the person or organization you are selling to. You need to watch what they need, what they already have, their income, and what they can afford. You need to be perceptive and watch what they reply to your proposals.

Who is a Salesperson?

According to wikipedia, a sales person is someone who works in sales, with the main function of selling products or services to others either by visiting locations, by telephone, or in a store/shop.

Salesperson is a broad term that engulfs many things. Sales people can work in a variety of ways. A salesperson can sell directly to customers or to other businesses or organizations. Many salespersons sell things in person, such as at a retail store or dealership. Moreover, the sales people commonly sell things over the phone or by communicating with people online as well.

In the 20th century and still today in some parts of the world, it was common for some salespeople to travel door-to-door to make sales to people at home. This led to the term door-to-door sales person. A salesperson who has to travel as part of his job can be called a traveling salesperson.

Figuratively, a salesperson is sometimes used to refer to someone skilled at persuading people, especially in a business or professional setting, as if they are selling them a product. This skill or quality is what we call salesmanship. This is an important skill in sales and in life generally because you have to convince others about your plans or ideas every now and then.

A salesperson's job is to sell and to sell; they have to convince the customer to buy. For that reason, salespeople have a reputation for sometimes being aggressive or putting pressure on the customer, especially in retail settings, like furniture or electronics stores. Moreover, this reputation is also because most sales persons work on commissions, a percentage of sales that goes into their paycheck. However, this shouldn't be taken as a negative thing, as many salespeople help you find the right product due to their skills as sales persons.

It is never too late to start; you can start today and take the opportunity available right now. Work as an individual for yourself, be only accountable to yourself, and make your dreams and aspirations come true. You can literally start with a pen and a contract and a commitment to excel at whatever you do. You can sell! No matter your personality type, anyone with a commitment can become great at selling.

Becoming a Great Sales Person:

People who are willing to commit to most selling as a career and are really interested in taking it to another level, will be greatly rewarded by this profession. They will continue to learn how to master this thing called selling and continue to learn new ways to reach higher levels of excellence. These people will be rewarded beyond their dreams.

Once you learn this great art of selling, you will never ever be without work, and you will never be without money. You will be needed! The profession of salespeople is needed more than any other profession. I frequently ask business owners about who they need the most. And almost every time, they say that they need motivated people who can produce. They say they don't need receptionists, janitors, website developers, or other technical workers. They say that these workers can be found in thousands, but it is all the front-end production that they need.

Business owners need people to sell their products or services in larger and larger quantities. They need people who can sell. If you get good at selling everywhere you go, you will be needed. Moreover, people who are good at selling will have no need to work for others; they can start their own. If you can control a sales cycle, you can have anything you want, go anywhere you want, and sell anything you want. Becoming good at sales is the key to all your dreams coming true.

To truly master the art of selling and applying sales in all aspects of your life, you will have to master some techniques that are a must for all salesmen. I learned these skills while I was throughout my career in sales. Once you master these techniques, you will no doubt become great at sales. These proven methods are described in the later part of this book.

Sales Define Business Success:

Customers buy products! That's what most people know about selling. Guess what is said to be the number one reason a business fails? The reason is that they do not sell enough, and quickly enough to the people who want to buy more than enough.

"The company ran out of money." You must have heard that statement. Think about it for a moment. If you are a professional salesperson who knows and understands sales and how to make it rain, then you know that the number one reason a business goes under is due to lack of sales. Who is in demand then?

Hence, when people say the number one reason a business fails is that the business was under capitalized; just say No! The primary reason a company, or an individual, or a management team fails is because they do not sell enough, and quickly enough to the people who want to buy more than enough.

In any type of business, the sales department plays the role of an intermediate, someone who bridges the gap between the customer and the business. When you go to a car dealership, who comes forward? A salesperson! The car salesperson will ask you different questions to get insights into your needs and wants and ultimately refer you to the right product for you. This helps both the business and the client because both benefit from the job of the salesman.

Another area where sales define business success is through customer loyalty and trust.

Loyalty and trust are the primary reasons the customer chooses to recommend your product/service to their friends and family instead of your competition. It is the main reason customers leave positive reviews instead of negative.

Reviews and recommendations are especially important today in the digital age. They have a huge influence on buyers' decisions precisely because the reviews are from a third party. During the sales process, good salespeople engage the customers so that they are impressed and are more likely to leave positive reviews and recommendations.

Sales also help increase customer retention for the business. Due to the personal nature of sales, it has a lasting impact on customers. Excellent salesmen not only make the sale but also manage to create long-term customer relationships, which are crucial for referrals and brand reputation.

The Importance of Commissions in Sales:

When talking to people about starting a business or sales, the most common thing that I hear is "commission." The reason this is always brought up is because of the mindset that has been instilled in everyone from a very young age which is to be safe, secure, and not take risks. But life and anything in life is a risk, and there is always a risk in anything that you do.
Ask yourself and others; what is the most common thing the highest-paid people in the world have? The answer; they generally get paid for the amount of business, revenue, or sales they bring in

Whether it is themselves or even a global sales team that brings them in, they all have the same common ground, which is someone needs to be sold or sell something to someone.

Having job security is great, and that's almost everyone's goal, but can you still be made redundant? Yes, you can be! Can the business still go under? Yes, it can! If you are in a non-sales role, not making sales, is it riskier than actually bringing in the sales? YES, it is. It is riskier to a company or a business that you are a fixed cost because then you have to rely on someone else to bring in the leads/sales so that you can do that work.

Ask yourself, are base salaries just as risky as sales roles? Yes! You have grown up with the belief system that you should become a slave to the system of worker bees and pay the taxes. You may be working harder than other people in your organization, but you have a fixed salary a lot less than theirs. Wouldn't you like to be rewarded for the efforts you put in? Sure you would! Are you even incentivized to work harder, smarter, faster, and with more efficiency? Sales roles are much more rewarding than base salaries.

Commissions are very important. They are a means to generate unlimited amounts of finances. Commission sales is the only way to separate yourself from not having everything you want and having everything! You want to have things, you want beyond commission, you want to have more things, and you don't want to be limited. If you want to own your own business one day, understand that having your own business means 100% commissions!

What are some types of commissions?

Even health is a result of production, eating healthy, and getting fit. Literally, anything in life can be tied to working on a commission. Don't be scared! Every business on the planet relies on revenues to continue to exist; your current workplace and the government relies on taxes.

Types of commissions can include recognition, promotions, raises, winning a contract, gaining new friends or business partners, and even getting a vote on a political election. Everything in one's life is a commission. If your business goes under, what happens to your job?

It's gone, isn't it?

You don't get guarantees in life; just like that, there are no guarantees in a commission and similarly in a salary job. Whether you want to start a business or be in sales or work for a company on an hourly wage, you will be on a commission. If you work your way up in a company long enough, you may even become a partner or director and then take a share in the business's revenue. Then the business sales will be the number one priority, and you can earn a small commission of the entire company.

People are often paid hourly because it's the cheapest form of payment for a service. You only get a commission for working hours and not on your productivity.? Salaries are not good for businesses because businesses are unpredictable; they sometimes make more money and sometimes not enough. That is why they have to rely on commissions, not salaries. If the company takes a bad turn, you go; that is why you're on commission. Why are you paid an hourly job? Because the other cost would be to outsource it!

Salary Vs Commissions, Which is better?

Whenever businesses, companies, or organizations take a downturn, who is the first person to lose their job? Is it the sales team members that are making the most money or the salaried people? The ones to go will always be the salaried people because the sales teams are the ones producing; they are the assets behind the business bringing in the revenue. If your business or the one you are working for isn't offering incentives to bring in business/revenues, you are missing out on the earning potentials of these people.

Salaries are the capped earnings. If you want to earn more or grow more, you need commissioned structures in place. That way, you control your earnings. Take a look at Amazon; they are paying people to drop shippers to use amazon to sell their products. Crazy right? People are earning millions through their own companies with Amazon, in the simplest form, that's commissions paid from Amazon as a sales person or what you call your own businesses.

Real sales professionals are able to hit the numbers that others cannot seem to achieve. If you can do this, you will be rewarded greatly. Making more sales and making lots of money gives you that confidence that comes from producing more. Then, soon you will be able to predict; the more you get done, the more you accomplish. And the more you know you can accomplish, the more you sell when you can sell.

The first sale is the hardest for everyone. Once you get past that, once you get the confidence and learn to predict, the next sale will be a piece of cake for you. When you gain some experience, your confidence goes all the way up. It's like you become magical; everyone starts to say yes to you now. You are on a roll or in the zone!

If you can produce more than the others, you can name your ticket, name your price, and you will be able to become more valuable than any salaried person on the marketplace. The business lifeline is all about production and revenues, meaning that the more you produce, the more you sell, the higher prices you sell them for, you can ultimately run the business, and you become the most important person for the business.

Another great thing about selling is that you need to understand the whole process from the beginning to the end. Whereas salaried people only have to learn about their specific line of work. However, if you're in sales, you need to know the business from the start to the end of the sales and know what's happening along that entire process. This makes you the single most valuable person to the business or organization.

The best thing I ever did in my life was to be rewarded for my efforts in my day-to-day work. It allows you to be free from overtime and free from limits that business places on your income. The only way to become financially free and to earn the lifestyle and money you want in life is to work on a commission and rely on sales and selling.

Moreover, there is one thing which is also important. And that thing is your relationship with taking the right action. Remember, each action that you take has a reaction to it, and it is that reaction that gives the results. Some people have an on and off relationship with action. This relationship is like an old acquaintance; it is good to see them, but the longer you go without seeing them, the harder it gets to connect with them. High achievers, no matter if they are on commissions or on salaries, have a strong bond with action and exclude everything else around. Funny enough, these are the people who get the results guaranteed regardless of their role as commissioned or salaried.

The volume of the sales affects the business, as stated before, not only volume but also the gross profit!

As a business owner and salesperson, you want to look deep into this; you want these two working together. What do I mean by that? Well, you cannot say that it's not in your hands to make profits because it is.

You control the percentage of how much you make every time you sell stuff!

If you think the opposite, you are wrong. It is a complete misunderstanding on your part. Even if you're not paid on the gross profit, you have to understand that each transaction has to accomplish profit in order for your company or organization to accept it as a transaction. Hence, you are paid on the basis of volume. It is based on the principle that the more items such as widgets, sticks, cars, furniture, refrigerators, TVs, or whatever you sell, the more profit you bring to the company or business, and hence you get more profit. How does the company dictate the price of the product you sell?

You, in a way, are linked to the gross profit your company makes. You may give discounts for multiple products, do you know WHY? Because you know that the cost of that sale was less! The only reason companies or small businesses fail, as mentioned before was,

It is their inability to sell products in quantities great enough and prices high enough. If you don't fall into that trap, you will never go out of business. If you want to own your own company, start your own company, or even work for a company. You need to learn this one thing. Sooner or later, you need to be responsible for controlling your volume and profit. If you want to own your own company, you better learn one thing; sell products in great quantities.

The same goes for services. If you provide more services, you make more money. Money is not the problem; management will help you with money. But sooner or later, you have to be responsible for your career. You will have to learn how to control both the profit and the volume in order to reach true levels of success in your life.

In our sales package and training course segments, we're going to cover a lot of information and techniques regarding both the value of volume and profit. We are going to teach you how to master these two. For now, I want you to learn this simple fact that commissioned positions are great! I don't know who told you they were not, maybe your dad, your mum, or somebody else. They may have been right to keep you safe and give you an average life with retirement, low healthcare, etc. But you don't have to be "just happy," you need to be more than that. Don't just be comfortable, be excessive, have high goals, and be excellent!

If you take a look at the world, you will realize that the industries are being wiped out right now, going bust, bankrupt, and being put into voluntary liquidation. What is the way out for you? It's Commission! Commissions are the only way for you to create financial security and stability for yourself.

Commissions don't confine you to a cap or a salary. Anytime you want to increase your income, you can! You only need to produce more! If you're mowing lawns for a job, either mow more lawns or sell for higher! That is the concept of volume and profit. Create more actions, improve approaches, and have a good attitude towards your job. Otherwise, you'll never get the volume and gross profits.

Do you want that safety net? With each week, each month, and every year having money in your bank. Learn your trade, master it, and keep learning. You should never stop learning and commit to it forever! Don't depend on a salary. Put all your trust in your personal abilities and be completely willing to do anything and everything to produce at higher levels. This is the basis for security, ITS YOU.

No safety net!

Partners of law firms, accountants, architects, and business professionals. Goldman Sachs, ballplayers, actors, and everyone else with big money on this planet are on Commissions! Hundred percent no safety! They may get a salary, but that is only based on the company's ability to produce. Control both, you have to control both, have high production and a high gross profit. If you can do these two things, you can control your income and bring it to any amount of financial freedom!

CHAPTER 2

THE SALES ECONOMY

Sales Drive Economy:

The economic growth of the entire world relies on sales. Consumer spending drives the entire world's economies. As such, retail sales is an important indicator. Think of it in terms of the products, companies, and people. The companies are involved in producing, distributing, and selling products such as food, clothes, fuel, and luxury items to people daily.

When consumers keep buying regularly, the economy tends to hum along. Retail shelves are emptied, and new orders are placed for replacement merchandise. Plants also make more widgets and order raw materials for even more production.

On the other hand, if consumers are uncertain about their financial future and decide to hold off on buying new refrigerators, or say, blue jeans, the economy slows down. This is exactly why

governments sometimes resort to tax rebates, and politicians run for office on the promises of tax cuts to boost the economy. By putting the cash into consumers' hands, they tend to spend their way out of an economic recession.

So what is the role of sales in that? Sales is an important part of that process. In order for companies and production businesses to continue to sell their products, they rely on sales and marketing to reach customers. Service providers are also dependent on their sales team to find prospective customers and reach potential clients so that a deal can be made.

Sales drive entire economies; I mean, they literally drive the planet. This is the most important role any salesperson has in the economy. Have you ever heard anyone say, "I'm just a salesperson?" If any salesperson says that, he is not aware of, or he does not understand the importance of his role, to the economy, to his family, to his company, and the entire world.

Successful salespersons are vital to the dynamics of every economy. Without salespeople, every industry on planet Earth will stop instantly. Salespeople are to the economy what writers are to Hollywood. No matter how great actors and actresses you bring in; if there are no good writers to write a beautiful story, the film will not succeed. Similarly, without great salesmen, even the brightest of the technical team will not be able to sell the products and reach customers.

What Happens when Sales Stop?

If you stop sales, what else do you stop? When the sales are slowed down or stop completely, the storage, accounts, logistics, advertising, and all economic activities are in turn halted. It can be stated that "The place becomes quiet."

The economic engine of every society relies on getting the products and services into the hands of buyers. Sales people drive products towards customers and, in turn, drive the entire economy. Sales people's job is more important than anything else. No economy will experience growth without salespeople. It's an amazing career and allows you to do what you want in life.

All aspects of businesses and organizations, such as storage, logistics, and advertising, are halted without sales. When the customers are not buying the products or

services provided by a company, the entire chain of transactions is affected and may collapse altogether. If the products are not sold regularly, the ones in storage may expire, leading to loss. If the sales aren't regular, the spending on logistics will bring back losses. Similarly, advertising will be futile as well without a great sales team.

There are very few sales courses at universities, and there is almost nothing in schools about sales. The limited knowledge about sales present in schools and universities is outdated and useless in today's markets. As such, we are missing the most basic foundation of growth and success from our education system.

Sales & Money

There is no shortage of money on earth, if you want to make big money, you need to know how money works. People usually are selling stuff but don't know enough about money. You have probably heard people say that "money doesn't grow on trees." What they mean is that money is in shortage. They are wrong! There is a lot of money on earth; it is unquantifiable. The money is printed by

governments, it's in excess; you just need to get connected to it.

There is enough money in the world to make every adult a millionaire in US dollars. But the problem is that no one is just going to give it to you. You will have to go and get your fair share yourself. Picture the ocean and the endless amounts of energy that generates. You could take as many buckets to the ocean, and it wouldn't make a scratch. Money is exactly like the ocean; there are tons of it. Don't believe for a second that money is scarce. You can be rich; you can be a billionaire, just like the more than 3000 billionaires worldwide. You need to handle the people around you. Stay away from people who don't believe in you and hang around with people who believe in you.

Salespeople are the most generous of all people because they don't believe there is a money shortage. Great salesmen know that money should not be sitting idle. It needs to generate more money. They know that money should be used and spent. If you can't spend it, then use it. Here is an advice, never save your money, rather invest it so that it works for you. When you invest it, it generates a cash flow and brings you more money in return.

What about boosting sales by 25% without selling an additional product? This is a great secret with sales and it is called second money. It is easier to get second money from the original sale. Maybe you have heard a phrase called value add. Once you have a sale, you can also open up the second sale by extending the sale to a further upgrade to inventory.

Have you guys ever bought a $100 bottle of vodka or wine or spent over $100 on a night out and complained about the steak being $30 at a restaurant?

What about movies? You get the ticket $15, then popcorn and drink is another $15 when you get there.

Additional purchases support the first buy.

How can you do this?

Wait until you are making the transaction, either with your card or via bank account, ask the customer if they want to upgrade. This will take the business margins to new heights.

How could you put in an additional value add service or add on to the customer that can boost revenue and margins?

Sales is a People-Business:

Salespeople need to repeatedly ask themselves this one question so that they never forget its importance. That question is, " What business are you in?"

And the answer to that question is, "You are in the people business." And do you know what the biggest weakness is in a people business? It's the people! Product knowledge and sales processes are great, but people are always first. Products and everything else is secondary.

1)   People
2)   Product

You are always in the people business, no matter what industry you are in. Therefore, your product should always be second to the people.

You have got to know your features, the benefits, and the competition. But it is the people who are more important.

It is important to note that selling is 80% about people and 20% about the product. Do you know why people buy inferior products every day? They buy milk from a servo. How much more inferior is that milk than the milk at woolies? Do you think they buy inferior products because they are cheap? Being cheap may be one of the reasons they buy these products, but it is not the only reason. It is the Conveniences, right?

Think of a shoe shiner at the airport. Don't you think people would look at their shoes and realize that they need shining? This is the time. So regardless of the product or the price. Advertise this "Shines over 60 seconds are free."

You're in the people business when I go to get my car serviced. When my tyres are shined and my car is freshly washed. That makes it just a better service than other places. What additional service can you add for your customers or can you do for your customers right now?

You need to speak in such a way that you make your sales process people-centered. It is okay to describe your services in a good and friendly way, but the ultimate goal should be the customer. It should be about the people, not about you or your company. It should be about solutions to their problems or needs and not about making money for your company. People are more interested in doing the right thing than what products they need. How much interest do you show your customers?

How can you be more interested? Is it genuine? 90% of salespeople don't take the time to find out what their customers really want. You need to take an interest in your customers and communicate with them. Right now, I am not communicating; I am just talking to you. Communication is the exchange of ideas and thoughts. It means that you have to listen to what each individual wants.

If the customers are not interested, you need to get them engaged and interested in what you are selling. Once you establish communication, you can present and close. You need the information to be understood and transferred; talking just about your product or service is not communication; it's talking. You need feedback, which can be turned into actions. You need questions that need to be drilled, trained, and rehearsed.

What questions would you ask your customers if you were to set up a survey for your customers right now? For people who have lost sales or are still waiting for them to be closed?

What are three things you can do today to demonstrate a willingness to the customer?

Why are there four seasons and hiltons? Are you a budget hotel or the Hilton?

If most of your customers are beating or shopping around for the lowest price, then your service is not obvious to them. They would not be shopping around and be willing to pay more. Don't blame the economy or the customer. Why do people stay at the Hilton? The more you're able to demonstrate your service, the easier you will be able to get money from a customer. No matter how service orientated, you still need to close.

Service is the way to higher prices, the way to higher profits, and the only way to less competition. Price is not a solution and is never the way out. Even a better product may not even constitute more money—ease of purchase, convenience, and not just price. People pay more for services than products. So how can you create a better level of service that someone will pay for? A buyer will pay more for great service.

1. Go to a client rather than them coming to you. Service sells, needs a person attached. Providing options.

2. Calling them back immediately and not waiting, not stalling, don't procrastinate, with urgency intention.

3. Sending gifts, flowers, notes, dropping by, smile and full attention, great attitude. Following up before and after, before there's a problem.

4. Not hiding, creative action where other people won't go or do. Being creative and thinking about new ideas of service.

5. Following up before and after

Let's come up with 3 new ideas now of how we can create more service.

■ There is no value for dropping my price

■ Problems are opportunities, all complaints are opportunities to provide a better service.

■ Most people don't buy without someone asking more than once, and someone isn't going to say yes if you quit on them.

CHAPTER 3

CRM & KPI
REPORTING FOR SALES SUCCESS

What is Customer Relationship Management (CRM) ?

Customer relationship management (CRM) is the combination of practices, strategies, and technologies that companies use to manage and analyze customer interactions and data throughout the customer lifecycle. The goal is to improve customer service relationships and assist in customer retention and drive sales growth.

CRM systems compile customer data across different channels or points of contact between the customer and the company, which could include the company's website, telephone, live chat, direct mail, marketing materials, and social networks. CRM systems can also give customer-facing staff members detailed information on customers' personal information, purchase history, buying preferences, and concerns.

Components of CRM:

Marketing automation:

This CRM tool can automate repetitive tasks and enhance marketing efforts at different points in sales for lead generation. E.g., If a sales prospect comes into the system, it automatically sends an email with marketing content and aims to turn the sales lead into a full-pledged customer.

Contact Center Automation:

This includes pre-recorded audios, chatbots, and other automated interfaces, which can cut down on the tedious aspects of a contact center agent's job. This helps the customer with problem-solving and information dissemination.

Sales Force Automation:

This tool helps track customer interactions and automate certain business functions that are helpful in following leads, obtaining new customers, and building customer loyalty.

Workflow Automation:

This CRM system helps businesses in the optimization of processes by removing useless workloads, thus employees are able to focus more on creative and high-level tasks.

Lead Management:

CRM can help track sales leads, thus sales teams are able to input, track, and analyze the leads data in one place.

Analytics:

Analytics is one of the most important parts of CRM. It helps increase customer satisfaction rates by analyzing user data and by creating targeted marketing campaigns.

Artificial Intelligence:

AI is extremely promising in identifying customer buying patterns, and it helps to automate repetitive tasks. One of its benefits is that it can predict future buying behaviors, and thus, it is very useful in policy making.

Human Resources Management:

CRM tracks employee information and performance data, which is very useful in managing the workforce.

CRM Technology types:

Large companies and corporations typically use these four CRM Systems vendors, Salesforce, Microsoft, SAP, and Oracle. CRM technology is of the following main types:

Cloud-Based CRM

This type of CRM technology uses cloud computing which is also known as SaaS (Software as a Service) or on-demand CRM. The data is stored on a remote external network that is accessible to employees from any place where there is an active internet connection. It is relatively quick, easy to use with limited expertise, and is cheaper. However, data security is a primary concern for the companies as they do not physically control the storage and maintenance of the data.

On-Premises CRM

With this CRM method, the company takes responsibility for the control, administration, and security of the database and information. The software resides on the company's own servers, and they pay for upgrades as well. It is a safer method for companies since they themselves take charge of the data.

Open-Source CRM

This is yet another CRM method. Within an open-source CRM system, the source code is available to the public, enabling the companies to make alterations at no cost to the company employing the system. This type of CRM system also enables the addition and customization of data links on social media channels, thus assisting companies looking to improve their social CRM practices.

What are Key Performance Indicators (KPIs)?

A Key Performance Indicator or (KPI) is a critical (key) indicator of the progress towards an intended goal (result). KPI provides a focus for operational as well as strategic improvement. It also helps in creating an analytical basis for decision-making and helps focus the attention on what matters the most. Peter Drucker has famously said that "What gets measured gets done." (8)

With the use of KPIs, managing the performance becomes quite easy. You will have to include setting targets (the desired level of performance) and then tracking the progress against that target. It often means working to improve leading indicators that will, later on, drive the lagging benefits. Leading indicators are precursors of future success, while lagging indicators show how successful the organization was at achieving the results in the past.

A simple example to understand KPIs:

Let's assume you wanted to use KPIs to help lose weight. Then, your actual weight is a lagging indicator, as it indicates past success, and the number of calories you eat per day is a leading indicator because it predicts future success. Suppose you weigh 250 lbs/ 113 kg (a historical trend called a baseline) and a person they would like to emulate is 185 lbs/ 84 kgs (comparison research is called benchmarking), they might set a 1700 calorie per day target (which is the desired level of performance) for leading KPI in order to reach the lagging KPI target of 185 lbs/ 84 kgs by the end of the year.

The relative business intelligence value of a set of measurements is greatly improved when the organization understands how various metrics are used and how different types of measures contribute to the picture of how the organization is doing. KPIs can be categorized into several different types: (8)

The Inputs

It measures the attributes (amount, type, quality) of resources consumed in processes that produce the outputs

The Process

This activity measure focuses on how the efficiency, consistency, or the quality of specific processes are used to produce a specific output; they can also measure the controls on that process, such as the tools or equipment used or the process training.

The Outputs

Are result measures that indicate how much work has been done and define what is produced.

The Outcomes

These focus on the accomplishments or impacts and are classified as Intermediate Outcomes, e.g., customer brand awareness (a direct result of, say, marketing or communications outputs), or End Outcomes such as customer retention or sales (that are driven by the increased brand awareness).

The Project

This measure answers the questions about the status of deliverables and milestone progress related to important projects or initiatives.

Another example to understand KPI:

Suppose my business provides coffee for catered events. Some of the inputs include the coffee (suppliers, storage, quality), the water, and the time (in hours or employee costs) that the business invests in. My Process measures could be coffee making procedure or equipment efficiency or consistency. The outputs would focus on the coffee itself (taste, temperature, strength, presentation, style, and accessories, etc). The desired outcomes would be customer satisfaction and sales. Project measures focus on the deliverables from any major improvement projects or initiatives, such as the new marketing campaign. (8)

CHAPTER 4

THREE PRINCIPLES OF EXCELLENCY; COMMITMENT, PREDICTION & CONFIDENCE

If anyone in any field of work can follow these three principles, their success is guaranteed 100%. These three factors decide whether you make that next sale or you will not be able to do that. They will get you anywhere in life. Opportunities present themselves only to those who are excellent at their work, and to get to excellence, you will need commitment, confidence, and the ability to predict.

There is a shortage of great salespeople in the world, just like the shortage of oil and water on earth. In a shortage like that, anyone who is great at what they do is extremely valuable. This is due to supply and demand. If something is in short supply, it has a high demand. If it is in high demand, people will pay any price for it. Great salespeople are in short supply today.

Today, there are millions of people who call themselves salespeople. Not all of them are great. To be a successful salesperson, you have to become genuinely excellent at what you do. You have to be committed, have a desire to be great, and have the dedication and willingness it takes to be successful. People are only limited by their imagination. There is actually no difference between making a million-dollar deal and a hundred-dollar deal; it takes the same energy.

You need to become the decider of your life, not your problems. Don't let problems dictate who you become. You have to choose where you work, how much you work, and when you work. Great salesmen think differently and act differently. They deal with their customers differently. Their work is effortless; why is that? Because they have put in the effort and have become the best at what they do. Take Tiger Woods as an example; he knows everything about each club.

It is said that it takes 10,000 hours of work to become the best at what you do. Why did I say that? Because no one is born great. They invest time and effort into it to be the best. They work so hard that, in the end, it is just effortless for them; it comes naturally to them. I have never ever met a successful person of any line of work that wasn't excellent at what he did. The world has a shortage of people like Tiger Woods, who excel at anything they do. Great salesmen make the sales look easy and inspire others to do the same.

The primary advantage of sales over other careers is that you don't have to depend on others to produce; they don't have to have a capped earning or salary. There is no limit in sales; there is no ceiling for your income. Even in times of global financial crisis or recessions, great salespersons and masters of sales will not fail; they will succeed because their income depends on their ability to create and they can create results.

Commitment Defines Success:

I have been fairly committed my whole life but never fully committed to anything as much as I am committed to selling now. I became fully committed! I was done pumping myself up because salespeople are pumped. That's just who they are; they don't need daily motivation; they should be motivated already. Do you have a sales team, or are you in sales yourself and you aren't pumped about your work?

Maybe you're doing something wrong? Do you have a sales team, and they aren't pumped to be at work? Well, then they're doing something wrong as well. Individuals need to be self-motivated. If not, then they are not great salespeople, they might be good, but they can even be higher if they're pumped. If you are wasting time pumping yourself or your sales team up, that needs to change.

My job is to convince you to be excellent; maybe I have done it already, maybe not. Maybe you are already great, but you need to give up your amateur life. If you have poor results or sales, we want to turn them around. What's the first step to being EXCELLENT? Commitment! Be obsessed; people will throw money at you if you are truly committed to something

The definition of Commitment is to devote oneself entirely to something. That could be anything. Marriage is a commitment! You are committed to not cheating, in sickness and in health, no matter what; that's commitment! Now, what are you committed to more?

Your marriage or your income?

What are you committed to right now?

What are the things you think you need to be more committed to right now!

Please read everything you can, consume everything you can, on this thing called selling. Make sure you convince yourself that this is your field and your chosen profession. This is the best thing that you have to learn to get your way in life. Selling is the thing which will make you rich.

How can you commit? You basically need to eliminate all other options and focus on this one thing. What you need to do is devote yourself to this one avenue only and forget about everything else. You have to become a fanatic and commit that you are not going to search any other way; that's it. Committing to sales is as simple as committing to a parking spot; you pull in your park, and you get out. You can't keep looking around for stuff. A firm final decision, you stop wondering, and you follow through.

Commitments cannot follow without an action to follow. Don't think about being an actor, a doctor, this or that. You don't think about it; just be devoted to the game. If you don't, you are never committed. Even if it is the wrong thing, at least you will find out. Quit wondering and follow through with your decision. Commitments can't take place without action. Don't pray; once you commit, you quit looking for other options. Could you find someone prettier or smarter in your relationship? probably, but that is not commitment. Write this down, "Commitment means you're in it all the way." This is important if you want to be a master at the art of selling.

Write down ways you're not committed! Write down ways you could commit more! Eliminate all other options!
I am sure everyone in the world has heard of the saying the grass is greener.

Everyone knows that the grass has to be always mowed. So it comes down to this, whose lawn would you rather mow?

Weeds grow everywhere. Stop looking at your neighbor's house and their grass. Stop looking for another job and commit to one job and excel at it. When there is greener grass on the other side, it means someone else committed, and now yours needs to be mowed. There are millions of people making money on the internet and millions that are not. Weeds grow if you neglect their feelings and don't mow.

When you neglect it, you will start to dislike it. Including houses, wives, cars, etc., the more you neglect, the more you'll dislike. Then you'll start peering over your shoulder and looking at better deals. You have to commit now and keep doing it. You have to realize that if you are not committed to what you are doing, not selling, sitting idle, then your grass will not be green.

The fundamentals are not product knowledge. You have to focus on selling and get committed to your career and get committed to being excellent. If you don't get that part right, you won't do anything on the other segments. We are going to get intense, but I have to get you sold. If you're doing this your whole life, 30, 40, or 50 years

and you're not getting results, then you need to recommit or commit properly and be honest with yourself.

You have to commit to selling your product and commit to learning everything there is about that product. When you do that, you will watch your sales increase immediately. When you commit properly, the results won't be late, and they will be big because committing completely and devoting your time to it is very rewarding. When you are doing a job, give your 100% to it, don't just hang around and see where it goes. Dive deep into it.

When I am with a client, I am 100% with the client; there is nothing else on my mind. I am not thinking about other customers; at that moment, all my energy is focused on this client only. At that point, I have to become a complete fanatic. Did I hear that right? Yes, you did, and yes, you have to become so involved in what you do that you become a complete fanatic. You must be insatiable about your commitment to get things done and go all the way.

Have you ever been committed to something so much that everyone else thought you were crazy? Recall and think about that action; didn't it totally pay off? I am sure the answer is, Yes, it paid off. When you give your 100% to something, it totally pays off.

When you want to stay committed to what you do all the time, you have to put reminders in place. These will constantly keep you focused on your goals and prevent you from wandering off the tracks. It is hard to stay committed. Therefore, you are going to use everything you have got to stay focused. One of the things that I do is that I don't dress for customers; I dress to impress myself. That gives me an edge and helps me stay committed.

At the age of 20-26, I was living a very uncommitted lifestyle. I was in and out of jobs; I was still looking for my parking spot and a girlfriend. I wasn't dug in and cut off from all other options, and thus, I wasn't getting any results. I wasn't proud of the work that I did and the person that I was.

I was merely an average, just like every other one; I was complaining about the market, economy, and everything else that went wrong.

I didn't have anything. Do you know why that was so? Because of the lack of commitment to life on my part. When you get results, that's when you like what you do. So, if you do the same, I guarantee you are going to be the same. Don't ever play a victim; get up and take charge of your life and sort it out the way you want it to be. Don't be confined to limits. Live free.

But when I committed, I instantly knew that I was doing so many things, taking so much action, and going after the things I always wanted. Back then, I only committed, I didn't know if it was the right thing to do, but I did it. I wrote a list and knocked everything down on that list until it worked.

To commit to sales, you need to learn everything you can. You need to video, record incoming calls, go to training, and any other venue where you can learn anything about sales. You have to put all you got into it so that you can stand tall over all other salesmen. At my first sales job, I studied and examined the top sales reps, analyzed, and kept doing everything in my power to be number one. Eventually, I was doing better than everyone else in the whole company.

Looking around, they were mediocre and average at best. They were not fully committed, and when you commit, you will get results. You need to start looking every day at how you can commit. When you commit entirely, your potential will explode. You will have a spiritual feeling that will make you feel above the rest. That's the magic of commitment: burn all the ships, so you have to go to land. You're all in, and that's commitment. All your chips are in the pot just like in poker; that's it, there is no coming back.

One of the first indicators I felt when I knew I was starting to become a professional salesperson was following that commitment. I became completely dedicated to studying the area of selling. I had so many notes. But it was when I went from being a salesperson to sales coaching that I really understood

sales. You have never actually understood something unless you can teach someone else. What you can't teach others you haven't learned yourself.

You can't teach people unless you KNOW. After I saw my results grow from reading, learning, going over the sales, much like a coach goes over the game, I gained my first real sales skill. It's called the ability to predict. See to predict means to know what's going to happen next. I didn't really think about it, but after a while, I knew like a poker player to start accurately reading people's cards. I felt my ability to predict outcomes and situations before they even happened, and I started getting better.

So I started to know exactly what I had to do each day. I started to know what people would say and do in response to what I said. Objections, questions, and closes improved. Indeed this is called the ability to predict. You have it; everybody has this ability. You've done it before; you've experienced in your life anything you've been committed to.

Your Ability to Predict Matters

Based on your knowledge of anything, you can predict results and to predict is to truly know something. Let's understand this with the help of an example.

If I could get in front of 10 people in a week, I could close three sales. If ten people would cost $x, then the total cost of sales would be $x. Then you can look at other numbers such as sales time. If I can get in front of 20 people, would that mean six sales? Can we improve any of these metrics?

Seeing the numbers and data is the next key to prediction. Once you're committed, you see more numbers, and you can make better key decisions with these figures. This became almost a natural thing; I was increasingly sure of what they would say, how they would react, what they would bring up, what they might initiate, even their thoughts and concerns that hadn't even come out yet.

I was starting to become aware and conscious that most situations are similar but not identical. This enabled me to predict objections, complaints, styles, and I was able to handle these before they even surfaced. When you're able to do that, you become the master of this profession.

When I mastered this, it was as if things slowed down, just like in a slow-motion movie. All great athletes have experienced the game slowing down. They were not only able to know what they would do but also able to predict what other players would do. By the time I could predict these, I loved commitment, and I continued studying and enhanced my prediction ability even further. At that moment, I knew that I had become a professional.

Prediction is a great unknown and unrecognized asset for career professionals.

There exists a phenomenon of some sort, most notably with athletes but with every professional who excels at what he does, where they are able to know exactly what is going to happen. I had never read about this phenomenon, nor had I seen a video or heard it from someone. But I know today that it exists, and I have experienced it multiple times when I am making sales. So how would you get this?

Well, first of all, think of it this way. When you are learning to ride a bike for the first time, how do you do it? You commit first,

improve your muscle memory, then you research by observing problems. Similarly, in sales, you observe the objections, problems, complaints, and anything else that stumps you.

Now think back to a time when you spent a long time doing something or with someone, and you noticed something familiar or the same with a certain person. You start noticing certain characteristics of those people. For some people, it is time. Certain customers are time-sensitive. A customer said to me once, " Oh! I only have 60 seconds," and I knew that these types of customers always say the same thing. I knew what to say. I said, "60 seconds is plenty of time for you."

So how do we increase our prediction ability? Well, it's like anything else; there is a science to it.

First, you observe, then you record.

What did the customer say?
What did the customer do?
What did he say?
What was your response?

Was that the best response, and could you think of a better response?

After a while, patterns emerge; patterns allow you to know what will happen next. Why is a pattern predictable?

How will that help you become a better salesperson?

For example, 3 customers say

"Don't have time" (Customer 1)

"You only have 60 seconds" (Customer 2)

"I am busy" (Customer 3)

Are they all saying the same thing?

The ability of prediction is the vital first step to becoming excellent. You have to understand that these customers are not saying the same thing. You have to understand the reason why they chose these words specifically because they're all in different situations. You have to dive deep and understand quickly what the customer wants.

The 1st customer is extremely busy and doesn't have the time to stay, so you don't have to provide many options, just point him out towards the best possible option, and that's it. The second customer has set a specific time parameter, 60 seconds. That means he has some time to look into options, but not so much time. Therefore, you need to mention 2-5 best options and let him choose. The last customer says he is busy, but he has sufficient time to weigh options. Therefore, you have to browse through a lot of options.

The ability to predict these small differences means a great deal in sales. It can be the difference between you making the sale and not making the sale. Therefore, you always have to practice and brainstorm different ways to predict what the customer is looking for

Confidence Goes a Long Way

Ask yourself this Question: What is a common thing in all successful people?

Your answer should be, "They are confident!"

Confidence is one of the key factors for success for all professionals. It is especially important in sales. You need

more confidence in sales than other professions because, in sales, you need to have confidence for you and for your customer. A lot of customers approach the purchase process lacking in confidence. This is because it is an unfamiliar "turf" for them.

That is the main reason your confidence goes a long way, both for you and for your customer. By engaging the customer confidently, you not only make the sale but also increase the confidence of your customer through their interaction with you.

Causes of Lack of Confidence in Sales

Lack of confidence is a true monster; it is devastating not only in sales but also in life generally. It leads to a recurring cycle of disbelief in one's abilities, which leads to a lack of confidence itself. The primary reason why people start to dislike sales and are not confident is due to the fact that they don't KNOW.

People may think it's because of rejection; some people say it's because you're too lazy to be in sales and that sales require too much work. Other people think it's because they believe they don't enjoy talking to people they have never met or that they might not like them.

The single reason someone doesn't like what they are doing is almost always because they don't know what they're doing right or what they're doing wrong. When you learn what to do and how to do something, there will be no way you won't like sales.

If you are not winning, why would you like it? It is as simple as that. A doctor who can't save lives, a teacher who cannot teach, a police officer who can't arrest people or stop crimes. Do you think they like what they're doing? No, they won't like what they are doing. Similarly, salespeople who can't sell won't like selling. So, What is the solution to this problem?

If your teams can't close, why would they be happy and motivated? Why would they follow up with prospects? It's not because they are lazy; it's because they just don't know. Whenever someone is not achieving their best, it can be as simple as that; they don't know how to achieve their best. When you don't understand something, that thing is not in your control, and without control, you don't get results. This is exactly why people start disliking their job because they're not in control and are hence unable to get results.

So, what is the way out?

The solution to lack of confidence is that you focus your attention on knowing what you don't know and understand what you're doing. Don't ever believe that you are lazy or that you are not cut out for sales. Don't be afraid of failures; they are necessary for your success. You must not let failures stop you; you must be motivated to keep moving forward no matter what.

You cannot build and maintain confidence without committing to excellence. Building confidence requires effort and dedication. The way out of this situation is to follow our program designed for you to grab any answers you may have. You will have to follow these three principles to find the way out of such situations.

1)   Commitment
2)   Observation
3)   Intense training

The first step to building confidence is always "Commitment." You must commit first, even if you don't know anything. You must say, "I am going to do this, period."

That is commitment; everything else is secondary to that. Commitment must not be confined to just wishes; you must act as well. You have to get there and observe everything deeply, what the customer's interests, fears, and all other factors related to him closing the sale. One factor that almost everyone forgets is the training, the intense training that it requires to excel at sales. Intense training is the best way to keep your commitment and is, therefore, crucial for success.

Look at Mike Tyson's early life. He was so incredibly committed!

During a discussion with EMINEM, Mike Tyson had this to say about commitment.

"Commitment is almost like; you have to give your happiness up to accomplish a goal. If you wanna be the best, obviously you can't collect it anywhere. If you wanna be the best, there are going to be disappointments. There is a lot of competition, there's gonna be a guy who peaked at a younger age, and he's gonna blow you away when he's a kid. And then you gotta deal with a guy who is gonna blow you away when he's an old guy. And then it's gonna come to a time when you're experienced enough; the next thing you know, you're still blowing everybody. So everybody gets their turn; that's the way it is. As human beings, what we do is avoid fighting all our lives."

You need to train daily, train, rehearse, and role play until you K.N.O.W! And you can handle every situation. You will have enough information from this course on how to handle every situation. You will love selling after this course, and you can use it not only in your sales career but to get anything and everything you want in life.

Because we all need to sell, and we all have to sell to get something in life.

How Do You Raise Your Confidence Level?

Now you may ask, "How do I raise my level of confidence?"

Trust me when I say this, you cannot build your confidence by just willing confidence. It can't be gained by just looking in the mirror and repeating motivational quotes or affirmations (they make you feel silly anyway). Confidence is built by bringing Belief & Mastery together.

Believing in yourself and in your abilities is the primary requirement for confidence. When you believe strongly in what you are doing and why you are doing that, confidence will be built in no time. Of course, belief alone is not sufficient; you also have to work hard to acquire the accompanying skillset. But belief comes first. When you can put these two together, the result will be high confidence.

Think about your sales presentation, which you are currently comfortable with. And focus on parts in that presentation which you can't wait to get to. It can be an objection that you can address, or it can be anything else that you are very keen on discussing that you can't wait for that part of the presentation.

Why is that so? The reason you are so interested in that is because you know you do that very well; that is why you are confident. You truly believe in what you're saying, and you also know that you have mastery over it.

One very useful way to raise your confidence level is to focus on one thing at a time and not think about your entire sales profession. Simply pick a specific area and think about ways to increase your confidence in that specific part.

Think for a moment, and ask yourself, "What is the primary requirement that I need to increase my confidence in this specific area? Is it belief, or is it mastery?"

Bear in mind that if you do not have a strong belief, then no amount of mastery won't suffice for anything. Therefore, it is useful to start with the belief. Make sure you understand your value and the reason that you are doing it. When you are sure about your belief, then move on to mastery and technique. Both of these work together to enhance your confidence. Confidence is the key to success and also changes your customer's world for the better.

CHAPTER 5

THE SCIENCE OF PERSUASION

Mihaly Csikszentmihalyi's "Flow"

Have you ever heard of the zone? Or being in the ZONE I have said it a lot, some other people call it the flow.

Psychologist Mihaly Csikszentmihalyi defines "being in the zone" as "flow"

"There's this thing about focus that, once it becomes intense, it leads to a sense of ecstasy, a sense of clarity: you know exactly what you want to do from one moment to the other... Sense of time disappears. You forget yourself. You feel part of something larger." (9)

According to this model, the secret to getting "in the zone" is the Goldilocks principle: not too hot, not too cold. You want to feel inspired but not overwhelmed. We can apply this to anything (everything!).

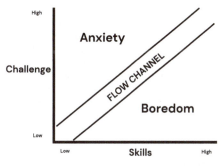

(The Flow. After Mihaly Csikszentmihalyi, The Flow (1990), p. 74)

Your squat weight, your career path, and your sex life: not so much challenge that you burn out, not so little that you get bored. (10)

Another thing to note is that the more you know, the more you can accomplish, the more you sell!

Consistency is a must in the sales business. You need to continue to make sales, and you need to make good sales. Each sale that you make must be approached with the same enthusiasm. You have to be good consistently, not just once or twice. You cannot afford to be bad consistently.

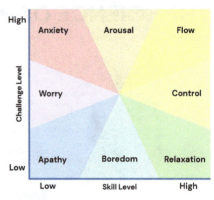

Csikszentmihalyi's Flow

6 Shortcuts to Persuade Anyone

Your ability to persuade others is the most important skill you'll need in the sales business. It is the most powerful skill of all for any sales professional. The skill of persuasion is required in sales and comes in handy if you want to lead and in defining your success in work and life generally.

Now we will discuss six universal principles derived from research done by the famous Psychologist Dr. Robert Cialdini and others in his team. These six principles are frequently employed by career professionals and world leaders to successfully influence others. The six principles are:

1. Reciprocity
2. Consistency & Commitment
3. Consensus
4. Liking
5. Authority
6. Scarcity

6 Shortcuts to Persuade Anyone

1. Reciprocity
2. Consistency & Commitment
3. Consensus
4. Liking
5. Authority
6. Scarcity

1. Reciprocity

An interesting concept to persuade people is reciprocity and is, therefore, the first on Dr. Cialdini's list. Reciprocity points out the obligation that you feel to give someone after you have received something from them.

This tendency to return a kind gesture or favor is an important principle to remember in order to understand persuasion, as can be seen in an experiment conducted by behavioral scientist David Strohmetz and his colleagues. In the experiment, customers at a diner, after finishing their meal, were given free mints with their bills. The experiment was broken down into three trials:

1. In the first trial, customers were each given a single piece of candy.

2. In the second trial, customers were each given two pieces of candy.

3. Finally, in the third trial, customers were each given one piece of candy. Then the waiter left the table; however, before the waiter completely left the area, they came back and gave the second piece of candy to each customer. Through this gesture, it was almost like saying, "...oh, for you nice people, here is an extra candy each."

Each trial also included a control group, which were given no candy with their bill. The results from the trials were:

1. For the first trial, the diner noticed 3.3% increase in tips compared to the control group.

2. For the second trial, the diner received 14.1% increase in tips compared to the control group.

3. For the third and final trial, tips increased by 23% compared to the control group.

The experiment concluded that people are more reciprocatory after they have received something. Additionally, the way in which they received that something influenced the outcome. Such as in the third trial, where customers at the diner tipped more after it appeared the waiter made an exception for them.

2. Commitment & Consistency

The second principle of persuading people is commitment and consistency. People are influenced or persuaded by you when you are consistent in your interactions with them, and they tend to move away from you when you are not consistent. Consistency is important for predictability, and people like predictability.

Social scientist Anthony Greenwald conducted a social experiment with potential voters on election day eve in 1987. He asked them whether they would vote, to which 100% of participants said yes. On election day, however, he found out that 86.7% of those who were asked had cast their vote as compared to 61.5% of voters who had not been asked that question.

This highlighted that people who publicly committed to voting were, in fact, more likely to vote. This is the tendency to commit to what you say; hence it is a universal principle of persuasion. When people make a commitment, they are likely to follow through with an action or decision to remain consistent with their commitments.

3. Consensus

People need approval for their actions and decisions and therefore look to others for guidance on their own matters. Dr. Cialdini and his colleagues conducted an experiment. They encouraged visitors to an Arizona hotel to reuse their towels.

Four types of signs were used to conduct this experiment. Each of the four signs encouraged visitors with a different statement.

1. The first sign cited environmental reasons to encourage visitors to reuse their towels

2. The second said the hotel would donate a portion of end-of-year laundry savings to an environmental cause

3. The third sign said the hotel had already given a donation and asked: "Will you please join us?"

4. The fourth and final sign said the majority of guests had re-used their towels at least once during their stay

At the end of the experiment, the percentage of those who reused towels per request were tallied:

Cialdini's Social Proof

TThe experiment concluded that when guests found out that most people who stayed in the same hotel reused their towels, they were more likely to comply with the request because they had a guideline to base their actions and decisions on.decisions on.

4. Liking

The next shortcut to persuasion is referred to as Liking, and the following was extracted from a publication called "Dr. Robert Cialdini and six principles of persuasion" by Tom Polanski, EVP at

eBrand Media and eBrand Interactive:

"People prefer to say 'yes' to those they know and like,"

Cialdini says. People are also more likely to favor those who are physically attractive, similar to themselves, or who give them compliments. Even something as 'random' as having the same name as your prospects can increase your chances of making a sale.
The article went on to detail a study that was conducted:
In 2005, Randy Garner mailed out surveys to strangers with a request to return them. The request was signed by a person whose name was either similar or dissimilar to the recipients. For example, Robert James might receive a survey request from the similarly-named Bob Ames.
According to a study reported in Yes!, "Those who received the survey from someone with a similar-sounding name were nearly twice as likely to fill out and return the packet as those who received the surveys from dissimilar sounding names (56% compared to 30%)."
After the study, the article explained that salespeople could improve their chances of making a sale by becoming more knowledgeable about their prospects' existing preferences.

5. Authority

The fifth shortcut to persuasion is Authority. People respect and trust authority and often seek the lead of credible experts.

Being in a position of authority or giving the appearance of authority increases the likelihood that people will comply with a request.

For example, the following was extracted from a 1974 experiment conducted by Stanley Milgram, Psychologist at Yale University:

[an experiment] where ordinary people were asked to shock 'victims' when they answered questions incorrectly. Those in charge were dressed in white lab coats to give the appearance of high authority. The participants were told that the shocks they gave increased 15 volts in intensity each time the person answered incorrectly. In fact, the shocks were completely imaginary. Respondents were acting.

As participants continued to shock their victims, the respondents feigned increasing discomfort until they let out agonized screams and demanded to be released. Astoundingly, about two-thirds of participants ignored these cries of pain and inflicted the full dose of 450 volts. According to Stanley Milgram:

"...the real culprit in the experiments was the [participants'] inability to defy the wishes of the boss, the lab-coated researcher who urged and, if necessary, directed them to perform their duties, despite the emotional and physical mayhem they were causing."

The experiment showed that people in authority have incredible influence on others, and when correctly incorporated, this influence helps persuade others to make a decision.

6. Scarcity

The last and final of the six shortcuts to persuasion is "Scarcity."

This shortcut can be easily understood with an example.

In retail stores, there are often sales for limited periods such as weekends or celebratory days. Why do you think that is so? The answer to that is the scarcity of it. The scarcity of this opportunity for purchasing a product at a discount actually encourages people to buy.

For example, the following was extracted from the aforementioned publication titled "Dr. Robert Cialdini and 6 principles of persuasion" by Tom Polanski:
In 1985, the Coca-Cola Company made their infamous switch from their traditional formula to the sweeter formula "New Coke." Their taste tests indicated that 55% preferred the new Coke over the old. Most of those tests were blind, but some participants were told which formula was new and which was the original. Under those conditions, the preference for new Coke increased 6%.

Despite the taste tests, the switch to the new Coke triggered an incredible backlash against it. Time magazine later dubbed it "the marketing fiasco of the decade."

"The company must have looked at the 6% difference between blind and non-blind preferences and said to themselves, 'Oh, good, this means that when people know that they're getting something new, their desire for it will shoot up.'" (12)

In fact, what that 6% really meant was that when people know what it is they can't have, their desire for it will shoot up. Later, when the company replaced the traditional recipe with the new one, it was the old Coke that people couldn't have, and it became their favorite.
The experiment showed that people are more likely to seize an opportunity if they know that opportunity is limited. Utilizing this principle, people are more likely to be persuaded if what is presented to them is rare or if they feel they will not have a chance at this opportunity again.
Next time you have a critical presentation, sales demonstration or startup pitch — stop and think about how you can be more persuasive with your message.

CHAPTER 6

THE PITCH (YOUR "WHY")

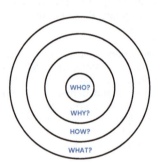

There are four fundamental questions that need to be answered for your customer. These four questions define your core and will provide all the basic details about your business, organization, or company that the customer is interested in finding. These four questions are simple and to the point; they are "who, why, how, and what."

In order to convince others to buy your product or whatever you are selling, you first have to be reasonable, believable, and above all, you have to sell yourself first. You first have to ask yourself, will I buy this product that I am selling? That way, you will be able to look at what you are selling from the customer's point of view.

The way I know people don't understand the game of selling is when I can see they are not completely sold in a product or service themselves in that company. You can see them and the company suffering. You've got to convince yourself that your product, your company, your services, and your ideas are superior to all others.

There's always going to be some competition, right? You have to be sold not just on the product but also on the service provided by the company and how you're going to support it. You have to be 100% certain on this idea that you're selling what you're selling and that your company is better than every other option out there. You have to convince yourself so much that you're almost fanatically believing in yourself and in your company or service. Don't for a second let the thought enter your mind that anyone else is going to compete with you.

It's you! It's the salesperson's job to create trust. Salespeople make sales. That's you! Whether you like it or not, you're handling people, not just selling something. If you can understand the mind, you can understand the customer. Never blame the customer; it's never the customer.

The customer says, look, I'm not buying anything today. I said if you don't buy anything, it's not your fault; it's all mine. We need to take responsibility for the sale, the buy, the management of the transaction. Don't just think about your role; think about what needs to get the job done.

People who say I am not buying today when they walk into that store are reactive comments. But   how often have you said you didn't want to buy anything that day and did anyway. When a buyer comes to your business, the only thing they should ever need to do is pay for your services. Whatever the stall or objection of a customer. It all comes down to trust. Even the buyer lacks their own trust in themselves to make a decision. But you need to come to an understanding with them.

When waiters at a restaurant give dessert menus, they have a more likely chance someone will buy dessert. Don't ask if they want a menu, just give give give!

Simon Sinek is the author of "Start with Why" and the creator of a concept he calls "The Golden Circle." The Ted Talk he gave on the topic is incredibly popular, with almost 10 million views as I write this.

Sinek's Golden Circle hits on some core truths and is almost right.

Sinek purports that great organizations seem to create their foundation by first addressing Why they exist, then How they go about their mission, and then finally, What they do.

Let me say first that I really appreciate what Sinek is doing — inspiring leaders to think about the soulful calling of their organizations and to rally others to a bigger cause beyond just selling widgets. And he does a masterful job of calling out that people don't buy what you do; they buy why you do it and that it's critical to attract customers who believe what you believe.

However, the truth is that great organizations build their core ideology by first defining and reinforcing Who they serve and the customer problem or need that they solve in the marketplace. Then they address and reinforce Why they exist, then How they go about their mission, and finally What they do.

So a modified more accurate Golden Circle should really be drawn like this:

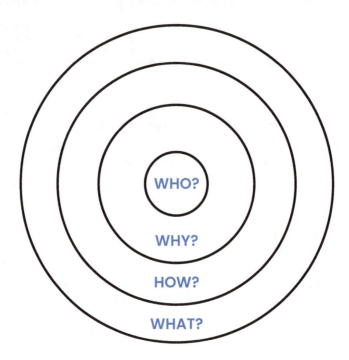

How do I know? Two reasons:

1.   A business doesn't exist to promote its beliefs. It exists to produce results for its customers (Who it serves). Understanding who your customer really is and the problem or pain they seek to solve is what differentiates a company in the marketplace and keeps it focused on the highest goal — creating customers.

It's an easy trap to fall into. You get so caught up in your own beliefs — how you think the world should be versus how it really is — that you lose sight of who your customer is and the pain point that they really want to be solved. That's why you exist, to solve a need in the marketplace. If you're not solving needs, then you're quickly going to go out of business regardless of how inspiring your vision statement is.

2.   Leading with Who is what also allows the business to successfully navigate what in his Ted Talk Sinek calls the "Law of Innovation Diffusion." This law is a term used to describe how innovations spread in the marketplace through a series of unique stages of customer groups. It tends to be depicted in a bell curve.

The sales pitch is designed to persuade a prospect to buy; your rep should know it inside out. While you review it, break the pitch into three parts: beginning, middle, and end.

With Clarity, certainty, and capability, you can achieve these goals together to make $.

"What is your Target Market? (Who)

With what Framework do you help them? (What)

What's the result or goal you wish to achieve? (Why)

What problem do you solve? (How)

Now let's put that into one sentence or elevator 30-second pitch for you.

We/I help (Target Market/Who) using (Framework System/What); it's a new way to achieve(Result/Goal/Why) by (Solving Problems XY/How).

Then to further this, you can add another why for more impact!

That way, you can do (Dream Desired Outcome or Alternate Goal/Why)

CHAPTER 7

POSITIVITY IS THE KEY

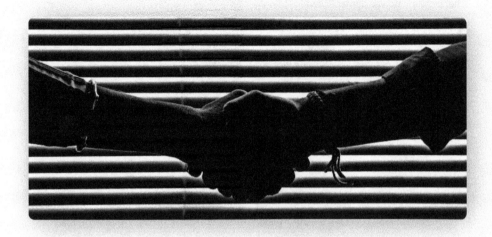

The most common rule of selling; if you want an agreement, you have to be agreeable. This rule is not to be confused. Don't confuse the saying the customers are always right. This is wrong. The point is that you agree. Agree while you're negotiating. Agreeing is necessary to get the deal done. People are attracted to things they are in agreement with. People move towards an agreement, do you agree? The people you hang out with are more agreeable with you.

Opposites do not attract, here is more evidence old ways are not the way to do things. Most people think it takes two people to have a disagreement or two to tango. But it really only takes 1 to agree; if they agree, there wouldn't be a disagreement in the first place. No matter what or how crazy some customers sound, whether they say this is black and it's white, you need to see from his point. But you need to agree with them no matter what.

Trust Leads to Positivity

What's the first rule of selling? Suppose a customer says, "I want to wait; this isn't right," when an agreement is already in place. What do you do? Let's practice this. Practice agreeing for one whole day or even a week to whatever people say and make a

sincere effort, and you will see some changes in your life. If you fail, start it again!

Unethical salespeople have ruined what it means to be in sales. Consumers are skeptical, and that puts people on guard before you may not even be able to gain trust. Distrust is not the buyer's problem if they don't believe what you say or your saying. Some distrust in you causes the decision to shop around. Always get a decision from the customer. Sleep on it, wait till tomorrow. Anything like that is a decision.

People believe what they see and not what they hear.

Help the customer make a decision, it is hard for them. If they think the price is too high and that they cannot afford it, they will choose another company. If they do choose someone else, it is because they don't trust you. By not making a decision of some sort, it creates a future problem and wastes time. You have to look behind the scenes and be responsible for the customer's mind, thoughts, reasons, and purpose. Trust is everything, if you didn't land a sale, there was no trust.

A lack of trust costs sales. Distrust costs you credibility, adds to the sale cycle, reduces your chances and overall sales amount, and drops margins for that sale. You can be trusted but still, lose credibility. I'll give you an example, running back to check with others. That means they lack trust. If you say, "I am not sure, I don't know." Appearing as a professional gives them reinforcement to make a decision. If you misquote something and give the wrong info, and they check online to see if that's true, then it will be very hard for anyone to trust you.

Then when there is an element of distrust, credibility is very difficult, no matter what you do. So you have to handle this distrust. And when you do gain trust, you need to appear credible. You could be really credible, and the buyer might have some false or misinformation, and then those two things collide, and you lose credibility. No trust, no sale, no credibility. This is not SELLING! We want to go beyond sales. You want to be excellent, and you don't get challenged when you are excellent; you build trust and keep credibility. These are two separate things, and they work together. Great salespeople understand distrust and make it their responsibility. How do you work on credibility? This means you need to know everything about your field, people, products, and competition. I don't just want to teach you how to sell; I want to make you a master to sell.

Have any of you had a customer look like they do not understand a single thing about you? The buyer already assumes he can't trust you. People will take the written word out of the newspaper because it's written and not what they are told. Presentation, proposals, products contracts all need to be in print. People have more trust and belief in written words.

Suppose you need something to show to a client, either in person or in an email to look at.

Assume that your buyer doesn't believe you. Buyers draw off past experiences of their own.

Validate everything you have with Data.

Doesn't matter how much of a perfect person you are; it doesn't matter. It's about the person and their trust. You need to have credibility and trust; the last 50 years of your life doesn't matter regardless of how trustworthy you think you are. Disbelief and distrust are real; that person has nothing to do with you. You can't just say to people, "yeah, trust me." It doesn't work that way. You need to show them, with something, paper, emails data. They are worried about being ripped off.

People misunderstand each other all the time. How do you tend to handle it? It's very easy to miscommunicate to understand someone. Sometimes it takes more than one time to communicate with someone. Words get lost, how to get credibility. You put it in writing!

Have you had any miscommunication or misunderstanding about anything?

Is there anything that we are doing right now that we can put in writing or give to the customer?

Do you use third party data in your sales process?

You don't want to shy away from contracts, agreements. I have heard people say, don't give them contracts or don't let them read T&Cs. Everyone knows everything. Signatures and contracts are your tools. There's never anything to hide from anyone. We are taking care of people, right?

10 Tips to Sell

1. Never sell with words.

2. Never negotiate with words.

3. Never close with words.

4. Never make verbal promises.

5. More data the better, don't be afraid to use as much info as you can.

6. Keep data and info current.

7. Have all written information available instantly.

8. 3rd party sources.

9. Make it easy for the customer to do research with you now not later.

10. Encourage clients to look at the information with you on the phone.

Your Attitude Is Important

A great attitude is worth more than a great product; people will pay more for a greater experience than a great product. Who doesn't want to feel good about being acknowledged or agreed with? People want to feel good. Positive people do this way more than the product of your service.

If you have a great attitude and great product or service, then you will exceed sales. By having a positive attitude, a person will spend little on necessities but more on entertainment because people want to be entertained. Why does Robert Downey get paid so much? Because people want to be entertained and feel good, laugh; they want to have a positive experience. Are you providing a positive experience all the way through? What are some ways for instant gratification?

Food, drugs, alcohol, gambling?

People will spend money on what makes them feel good over what they need; it explains poverty levels, crime, and a lot of issues.

Let's do an example

If someone says, "That's expensive." What do you say?

I agree; when it comes to your representation, would you take the risk? What would you think of our service if we were the cheapest? I am very happy to help you with some other payment options such as..

When people are buying something, you want positive people. You want smiling, motivated people surrounding you.

The ability to see positivity in people, in yourself, and be positive will ensure you always look for the best outcomes in any situation you might see yourself in with a customer.

Attitude needs to be viewed as more important than anything else. It's a factor to the money can't buy happiness. It can't be because you have a bad attitude or a negative view of the world. You wouldn't care about money or what it can do if you have a negative outlook on life. Do you dislike it when someone is positive? It's pretty hard, isn't it? Does anyone here like being negative?

Look, this is something we all need to work on because life is negative, isn't it?

Who here would like a million dollars? What would you do with it?
Are you a little happier?

Well, you need to treat people that you speak with like they are rich enough to do anything they want. Treat them like they have money. People will spend more money. Don't assume anything about a person, about how much they earn or don't earn. Always assume people have money and they can always afford your service. No matter what age.

You have a customer, broke, out of work, can't finance anything. Need to treat these people like they do have money; you cannot make any judgments on someone or assumptions.

Have you ever felt a bit useless when someone assumes you can't pay for something? Take going to dinner, and you don't have any money. You feel bad, right? If your service is going to better the customer, then it doesn't matter at all because they will be in a better situation after. If you really believe in your service or product, wouldn't you do anything to ensure that person is helped?

Here is a good example.

A guy walks in to buy a phone and says, "Hey, look, I just want this phone. I don't need your help or assistance or recommendations."

I understand what he's trying to do, and I agree with him whatever he says. It might not
make sense right now, but he may change his decision later.

But since I knew that attitude is more important than the product or the price and I believe when they are
treated right, they will act a certain way. A positive attitude can change his mind later but for now, just
provide him with a fantastic attitude.

The same person says I can get this phone online for
way cheaper.

Once again, guys, what would you say?
I would say no problem, my man; whatever you want, it's yours; I just appreciate the opportunity to do business with you.

Let's work it out together; tell me what you want? Why do you want it? Let me make sure we can do it.

So someone says, look, I want to shop elsewhere, I want it for super cheap, you say.

"Leave it with me; I'll sort it out. We just appreciate your opportunity."

How can you change the experience here for the customers?

How can each one of you make the experience more personable with each one of you individually?

Did you build rapport with the customer, or do you pass it on to someone else?

Customers pay for you, your attitude, and your experience.

Simple people act how you treat them; I am sure you don't treat everyone badly. You can shop around for products or services, but what can you not shop around for?

Attitude and positive people.

Positivity through Persistence & adversity.

How do you change other people's attitudes? If you can change someone else's attitude into a positive one, do you think that can change the outcome of your situation? It will work regardless of your product or service being superior. It is an ability. Mental skill is a muscle. Like a gym, it needs training.

Now we look kind of crazy, aren't we? That's good. Look, bad habits create bad habits. Can't just walk around saying, ok have a good attitude; I am positive, I am great. You need to drill it, build muscle. You don't need to be crazy-sounding or sound insincere to a client.

You are a product of your environment. Anything that you do here or outside of work also affects you and will affect work. Do you agree?

Look around your environment. What is positive and what isn't?

Media is full of it; people feed off it. It's the reason the media exists; it's human nature. Warmongering, recession fears even the flu pandemics. People get the flu when they think they are going to get it. It's proven. What am I getting at here?

Well, everything affects you, negativity every day, so when a client hears you say, no worries, I can do that for you.

Tips to better attitude

1. Avoid Media

2. Avoid negative people

3. Tell everyone what you want and your goals

4. Physical health

5. Hospitals and Doctors are sick factories

6. Negative talk in office

CHAPTER 8
THE PRICE IS RIGHT

All surveys on salesmen say the number one objection they hear is price. But they are incorrect; in fact, it's not further from the truth. Now I need to sell you on this idea that it's not the problem, it's not the biggest concern, most sales are lost from objections never heard. Customers don't usually even tell you the reasons. Closing the sale isn't about money,

It's about confidence, about it being the

1. Right service or product,

2. Salesperson

3. And the company.

Decision making is the #1 problem

You would not sell your service for $10! You would go out of business, or they would think it's too cheap. If you think that price is the problem or paying upfront is the problem, you are wrong because your thoughts are the problem.

The customer simply isn't certain with,

1. The product or service
2. Sales Person
3. Company

It takes a human to sell the value presentation and get emotional and get the customer excited so they can make sense of the price. Customers need to make sense of the difference between what they believe a price is to your price. Logical reasons to make sense of the money need a decision first.

1. First is the decision before the price
2. Money

First step in any sale. You sell them emotionally and close with logic.

Price is never the problem; you need to look back and find out whether they have made a decision first before the price is even thought about. Before anyone should even pick up the phone, you need to believe that no matter what the customer says, that price is never the issue; you just haven't figured out the decision first.

If you are solving customers' problems throughout your sales process, you will resolve any price conflict. When there is a price conflict, there is something you don't know about what the customer values. If you don't know what they value, you cannot provide information to make sense of the price. You need to know what else is important.

Let's say your competitor has the same product, why would they pay more? You and your company are the only differences. Not the service; you need to give buyers a reason for you and the company. There is always something cheaper every day for anything.

But why do people not just buy from the lowest bidder?

You want more, right?

1. First make sure the customer loves the product.

2. Be Confident that it will solve their problem.

3. Why are you & your company different?

How do we know they love the service?

1. Determine connection by presenting other possibilities.

2. Scale of 1 to 10 how do you rate this?

Every customer is looking to solve a problem. How do we solve it?

1. What is the problem, primary motivation?

2. Why now.

3. Make people like you by servicing them and never quit building rapport.

4. Laugh and inspire, show them you care.

If you ever lost anyone special, you would pay anything to have that person back, right? That's love. You need the buyer to want your service more than their money..

What Is Intrinsic Value?

Intrinsic value is the perceived or calculated value of an asset, an investment, or a company. The term finds use in fundamental analysis to estimate the value of a company and its cash flows. Another use of intrinsic value is in the amount of profit that exists in an options contract.

Perceived Value

In marketing terminology, perceived value is the customers' evaluation of the merits of a product or service and its ability to meet their needs and expectations, especially in comparison with its peers.

Someone needs to believe the value of the product exceeds the value of the person's money.

1. Find out problem
2. How will it be solved

If the value in your service is high enough, the customer will come up with the money somehow. Remember to treat them like they have money.

Let's do this now with your services. Let's assign a price to it. How are you going to build a greater price in the product? What other concerns could there be?

The buyer might have other concerns that don't even involve money. Half the time, the price isn't even a problem because there just might be something you don't know about their concerns. Customers man think, is this the right product? Is there a better product? Is the proposal good? Will it solve the problem? Will I use it? What will other people think about this? Will this company really take care of us? Am I better off buying something else?

Lead Buyers in the Right Direction

The world is your competition. You can spend $50k on a car, a house deposit or fancy clothes or whatever. Heaps of stuff out there; what can you buy? Do I know enough? Should we invest this money somewhere else? These questions must be answered during the sales process, you need to identify these, but it's almost never about price.

Let's say you're buying a present for your girlfriend. And you go to purchase something, and you tell them the price. They say, "O woah, that's out of my budget." Boom! There you go, there's something else. It's because they're not sold on that product. Which will solve the problem you don't even know yet. If you address all these concerns, price won't be an issue.

A common mistake is always offering for a lower price whenever faced with a price objection with a way to resolve the price objection.

This is not why people don't buy things; when you move them down to something cheaper, they are less likely to buy and cause the buyer to believe you actually don't have a solution. To figure out the actual concern, you should move the buyer up and will get the customer thinking about value and can eliminate the objection completely. Let's say you are at the jewelry store now and you were offered a $6,000 ring after he says that's not in his budget, say to him look just for fun, have a look at this one for $10,000, what do you think? Buyers are more concerned about making a good decision regardless of the price.

If you have other products in your inventory, you start from the highest, getting him to move in the direction they want to go because if customers see the higher value item, they will see the value in the other price.

This also exhausts the need to shop around, exhaust your inventory, and do not exhaust your margins. You lose the same amount of customers to more expensive products than you do to cheaper products, don't try to beat the competition.

Buyers pay more for the right decision, so another thing you can ask is what product do you think is right for them? Don't buy into the price issue..

Don't Blame the Customer

So how can we move customers up? What solutions do you guys have that are more expensive?

Salespeople stop sales; customers don't! And you are the ultimate barrier to the sale. You need to take the blame; customers are not the problem; it's the team. Placing blame on the customer will never come to a resolution. It is critically important to stabilize things you can control, which is you! Never blame anything but yourself. You need to close the customers. If you don't know how to reason with people or negotiate, then you are the barrier. Never turn the responsibility to the customer.

CHAPTER 9

GOALS, GOAL SETTING & VISION

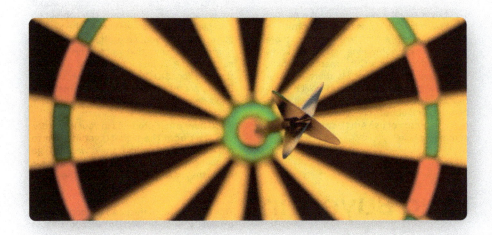

Sales isn't a job title; it's who you are. Whether you are a CEO, a manager, a business owner, or an entrepreneur, you need to be a great salesperson. It is vital for getting rich and successful with your life, business, and career.

Selling is a hard task, it doesn't come easy, and above all, it requires time, patience, dedication, and hard work. You have to learn how to sell not only in sales but also in your life generally. This program will help you uncover the secrets to getting good at sales with goal setting and vision.

When I started this thing called selling, I had no idea of the life it would lead me. I had no idea of the success you can attain with being a master at sales. Every job I have had since then was sales and grew and grew and grew. Each role was commission based, and everything I did was selling and negotiating. Being motivated is a form of selling. Everyone in the world doesn't realize that selling plays a pivotal role in their jobs.

The success you experience in your life will depend solely on selling. You need to sell even if you're a hairdresser. Without successfully selling, you won't go far. Most salespeople don't even know what selling is, and they can't even predict their results. If this offends you, hang out, and I'll be very surprised if you don't learn anything from this program.

You need to be in control of your customers, career, and income. This is an art, and you need to master it. Real pros see the mechanics in their minds and they don't even call themselves salespeople. Litigators moderatis, inverters, agents, entrepreneurs, actors, financial planners. JFK, Martin Luther King, Bill Gates, Martha Stewart. Masters.

Do you feel like selling is a pastime or a hobby?

Do you enjoy golf or your hobby more than you do selling?

Do you lack confidence selling?

Are you clear when you negotiate?

Do you struggle to get people to say yes?

Do you struggle with rejections?

Do you get argumentative?

Do you have a disdain for selling? Even a little bit?

Have you ever thought, oh my god, I have to sell something again or oh no, not again?

O, I don't want to pick up the phone again; why am I doing this?

Selling is crucial to life to get what you want. Decide right now to be committed. Prayers won't do anything. It's all on you. If you're not getting your way or what you want in life, then you need to be a master at this thing called selling.

Doing what you hate, what others won't do, will get you paid more than others. It's a lie that doing what you love will get you rich, or you won't have to work a day in your life. The things people don't want to do is where you want to be; that's how people become successful because they do things other people can't do.

Have you ever seen a painting that sold for a lot of money, and you think anyone could have done that? But you know what? They didn't! You pay people to serve you and do things others won't do and get paid for it.

Working on oil rigs, mines, all that sort of stuff, yeah, it gets you paid more because no one wants to do it.

The Difference between Vision, Mission, and Goals

Vision and mission are two similar but different things. You don't want to confuse one for the other. Vision is a clear mental image of what you want your business to be like in the future based on your goals and aspirations. When your business has a vision, it will have a clear focus, and it will help you head in the right direction and avoid you from getting off the track.

A mission, on the other hand, is the set of the core values and objectives that you or your business/company represents. A company delivers its mission to the consumers through a mission statement. The goals are objectives that the company sets to reach its desired vision and accomplish.

The Importance of Vision:

Many skills and abilities separate effective strategic leaders like Howard Schultz from poor strategic leaders. One of them is the ability to inspire employees to work hard to improve their organization's performance. Effective strategic leaders can convince employees to embrace lofty ambitions and move the organization forward. In contrast, poor strategic leaders struggle to rally their people and channel their collective energy in a positive, focused direction.

"Good business leaders create a vision, articulate the vision, passionately own the vision, and relentlessly drive it to completion."

—Jack Welch, former CEO of General Electric

As Jack Welch suggests, the key to inspiring the people in an organization is the vision from executives and leaders. An organization's vision describes what that particular organization hopes to be in the future; a well-articulated vision describes the organization's aspirations.

One limitation of such all-encompassing goals is that front-line and operational employees will not relate or connect with the goals and will disengage from the process – flavor of the month.... The CEO/management team who can effectively translate the high-level objectives to on-the-ground activities will have good success in engaging staff! Of course, a strong element of walk-the-talk is required by management as well.

The results of a survey of 1,500 executives illustrate how the need to create an inspiring vision creates a tremendous challenge for executives. When asked to identify the most important characteristics of effective strategic leaders, 98 percent of the executives listed "a strong sense of vision" first. Meanwhile, 90 percent of the executives expressed serious doubts about their own ability to create a vision. Not surprisingly, many organizations do not have formal visions. Many organizations that do have visions find that employees do not embrace and pursue the visions. Having a well-formulated vision that employees embrace can therefore give an organization an edge over its rivals.

Vision Statement:

Companies produce their vision statements to let consumers know of their aspirations for the future. This is the best way you or your business can communicate your vision, i.e., with a vision statement.

A vision statement in writing captures the essence of where you want to take your business. This inspires you and your staff to reach the established goals.

A vision statement communicates your ideal long-term business goals with your customers, and it reflects your view of the world and the place of your business in it. It answers the fundamental question, "where are we going?". Whereas a mission statement describes the practical aspect of that statement as, "How will we get there?"

The vision statement of your business or company should be inspired by real aspects from your business, such as,

- Your reputation

- Passion

- Service/Product quality standards (e.g. to make customers a priority)

- The growth of your business (e.g. you offer new products, innovate, get more customers, increase locations)

- Sustainability, going green (e.g. your company utilizes environmental friendly energy).

Your vision statement should also describe how you started and what inspired you to start this business, company, or service. It should also describe the values and principles that are important to you.

Mission Statement:

A mission statement, in essence, is a short summary of your company/business' purpose. It is defined as an action-based statement that describes your organization's purpose and how you serve your customers. Most of the time, a mission statement includes a description of the company, its objectives, and what it does.

A mission statement also provides clarity on the "what," the "why," and the "who" of your company. Ideal mission statements describe the guidelines by which the company operates. Mission statements should include all that the company does to accomplish its mission.

"Most mission statements are between one and three sentences, never exceeding 100 words. The best mission statements are typically a single succinct sentence, so keep this in mind when crafting yours." (13)

Your company's mission statement should be communicated to employees before their first day on the job. It should be highlighted on all your recruiting and onboarding materials, and employees should know it by heart. After all, this is the mission your employees should be aligned with every day. Otherwise, they'll come into work feeling aimless and struggling to understand their purpose.

Google's mission is to organize the world's information and make it universally accessible and useful (Edwards, 2012). Google expands on its mission by listing "Ten things we know," including "Focus on the user and all else will follow," "It's best to do one thing really, really well," and "Fast is better than slow" (Google Inc., 2014).

This brief but powerful statement emphasizes several aims that are important to Google, including excellence in customer service and setting high standards for employees and Google's products. McDonald's brand mission is:

"To be our customers' favourite place and way to eat. Our worldwide operations are aligned around a global strategy called the Plan to Win, which centres on an exceptional customer experience – People, Products, Place, Price, and Promotion. We are committed to continuously improving our operations and enhancing our customers' experience."

To be effective, this mission statement must filter down to all employees and inspire them to adopt that mission. (Edwards, 2012).

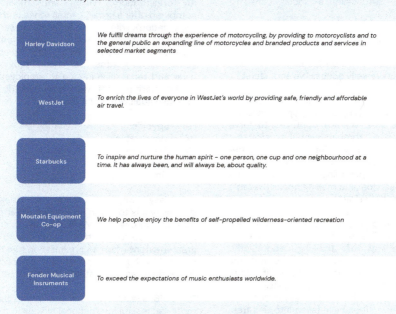

While a vision describes what an organization desires to become in the future, an organization's mission is grounded in the past and present. A mission outlines the reasons for the organization's existence and explains what role it plays in society. A well-written mission statement captures the organization's identity and helps to answer the fundamental question of "Who are we?" As a practical matter, a mission statement explains to key stakeholders why they should support the organization. The following examples illustrate the connections between organizations and the needs of their key stakeholders.

Harley Davidson	We fulfill dreams through the experience of motorcycling, by providing to motorcyclists and to the general public an expanding line of motorcycles and branded products and services in selected market segments
WestJet	To enrich the lives of everyone in WestJet's world by providing safe, friendly and affordable air travel.
Starbucks	To inspire and nurture the human spirit – one person, one cup and one neighbourhood at a time. It has always been, and will always be, about quality.
Moutain Equipment Co-op	We help people enjoy the benefits of self-propelled wilderness-oriented recreation
Fender Musical Insruments	To exceed the expectations of music enthusiasts worldwide.

At WestJet, Clive Beddoe and his team developed its mission statement:

"To enrich the lives of everyone in WestJet's world by providing safe, friendly, and affordable air travel."

A mission such as WestJet's states the reasons for an organization's existence. Well-written mission statements effectively capture an organization's identity and provide answers to the fundamental question "Who are we?" While a vision looks to the future, a mission captures the key elements of the organization's past and present.

Organizations need support from their key stakeholders, such as employees, owners, suppliers, and customers, if they are to prosper. A mission statement that engages stakeholders will help develop an understanding of why they should support the organization and clarify what important role or purpose the organization plays in society – also called a "social license to operate."

Google's mission, for example, is

"to organize the world's information and make it universally accessible and useful."

Google pursued this mission in its early days by developing a very popular Internet search engine. The firm continues to serve its mission through various strategic actions, including offering its Internet browser "Google Chrome" to the online community, providing free email via its "Gmail" service, and making books available online for browsing.

In ancient times, Aesop said, "United we stand, divided we fall." This provides a helpful way of thinking about the relationship between vision and mission. Executives ask for trouble if their organization's vision and mission are divided by emphasizing different domains. Some universities have fallen into this trap. Many large public universities were established in the late 1800s with missions that centered on educating citizens.

As the 20th century unfolded, however, creating scientific knowledge through research became increasingly important to these universities. Many university presidents responded by creating visions centered on building the scientific prestige of their schools. This created a dilemma for professors: Should they devote most of their time and energy to teaching students (as the mission required) or on their research studies (as ambitious presidents demanded via their visions)?

Some universities continue to struggle with this trade-off today and remain houses divided against themselves. In sum, an organization is more effective to the extent that its vision and its mission target employees' effort in the same direction.

Pursuing the Vision and Mission through SMART Goals:

An organization's vision and mission combined offer a broad, overall sense of the organization's direction. To work toward achieving these overall aspirations, organizations also need to create goals—narrower aims that should provide clear and tangible guidance to employees as they perform their work daily. The most effective goals are those that are,

(S)   Specific,
(M)   Measurable,
(A)   Achievable,
(R)   Realistic, and
(T)   Time-bound.

An easy way to remember these dimensions is to combine the first letter of each into one word: SMART. Employees are in a much better position to succeed to a greater extent when an organization's goals are SMART. A goal is specific if it is explicit rather than vague. WestJet's vision is that,

"By 2016, WestJet will be one of the five most successful international airlines in the world, providing our guests with a friendly, caring experience that will change air travel forever."

A goal is measurable to the extent that whether the goal is achieved can be quantified. WestJet's goal of being one of the five most successful international airlines in the world by 2016 offers very simple and clear measurability: Either WestJet will be in the top five by 2016 or they will not.

A goal is aggressive if achieving it presents a significant (as opposed to easy) challenge to the organization. A series of research studies have demonstrated that performance is strongest when goals are challenging but attainable. Such goals force people to test and extend the limits of their abilities. This can result in reaching surprising heights.

WestJet is committed to growing responsibly and ensuring that it is an environmentally sustainable airline and supports the IATA goal of carbon-neutral growth in its industry beyond 2020. WestJet already operates one of the most modern and fuel-efficient fleets in North America.

Achieving carbon neutral growth will be a challenge for WestJet, requiring the airline's combined efforts and supplier partners such as aircraft manufacturers, airports, and government. In 2012, WestJet reported that

"Our significant investments in fleet and technology have greatly improved our aircraft fuel efficiency and ability to operate our business more cost effectively. Between 2000 and 2012, we improved our fuel efficiency by 44.8 per cent per revenue tonne kilometre. The resulting fuel savings are equivalent to the amount of fuel that would have been used to fly a Boeing Next-Generation 737 from Calgary to Toronto and back approximately 44,135 times (based on our 2012 fuel usage)." (14)

It is useful to know that easily achievable goals are not only easy, but they tend to undermine overall motivation and effort by employees, Michelangelo said,

"The greater danger for most of us lies not in setting our aim too high and falling short, but in setting our aim too low and achieving our mark."

Consider a situation in which you have done so well in a course that you only need a score of 60 percent on the final exam to earn an A for the course. Understandably, few students would study hard enough to score 90 percent or 100 percent on the final exam under these circumstances. Similarly, setting organizational goals that are easy to reach encourages employees to work just hard enough to reach the goals.

While missions and visions provide an overall sense of the organization's direction, goals are narrower aims that should provide clear and tangible guidance to employees. The most effective goals are those that are SMART (specific, measurable, achievable, realistic, and time-bound). SMART goals help provide clarity, transparency, and accountability. WestJet's goal is "to enrich the lives of everyone in WestJet's world by providing safe, friendly, and affordable air travel. By 2016, we strive to be one of the top five airlines in the world as measured through key metrics such as on-time performance, safety, profitability, and guest satisfaction."

WestJet's goals fit the SMART acronym:

Specific:

WestJet strives to be among the top five international airlines. In contrast, "the best" would be vague, making it difficult to decide if a goal is actually reached.

Measurable:

WestJet identifies the key metrics: on-time performance, safety, profitability, and guest satisfaction. WestJet is able to measure its progress relative to its targets.

Achievable:

WestJet lists achievements to date in working towards the goals. A series of research studies show that performance is strongest when goals are challenging but attainable.

Realistic:

WestJet states support for the International Air Transport Association's (IATA) goals of a cumulative global average improvement in fuel efficiency of 1.5 percent per year through to 2020. Reaching a goal must be feasible for employees to embrace it.

Time-bound:

WestJet's timeline is 'By 2016". Deadlines are motivating and they create accountability.

It is tempting to extend this logic and thinking to conclude that setting nearly impossible goals will encourage even stronger effort and performance from staff. However, people act rationally and tend to become discouraged and give up when faced with goals that realistically have little chance of being reached. If, for example, Starbucks had set a time frame of one year to regain a share price of $35, it would have attracted scorn.

The company simply could not be turned around that quickly. Similarly, if WestJet's fuel efficiency goal were 100 percent improvement, WestJet's employees would probably not embrace it. Thus goals must also be realistic, meaning that their achievement is feasible.

Most of us have found that deadlines are motivating and that they help you structure your work time. The same is true for organizations, leading to the conclusion that goals should be time-bound through the creation of deadlines. WestJet has set a goal to achieve a cumulative 45 percent improvement in fuel efficiency for our 737 fleet by 2020, as compared to the 2000 base year. (WestJet, 2012)

The period after an important goal is reached is often overlooked but is critical. Will, an organization rest on its laurels or, will it take on new challenges? Starbucks provides an illustrative example. In 2011, after a revamp of the company's stores and services, the stock price was around $35. In early 2014, the price was in the $70 range.

How to Sell Yourself

1. Let's hear some success stories (let's write 3 success stories about customers now)
2. Build a manual on these
3. Stay sold on the product no matter what, if you are not sold ask yourself why
4. Buy your own products. Would you buy them for that price?
5. Be fanatical or almost crazy sounding to do whatever attitude it takes

If you don't want to do any of this, if you don't want to be this kind of person, then you won't get your way. Get sold and stay sold with ongoing training, rehearsing, and positive feedback from customers.

The Importance of Vision:

If you are not prepared for a sale or a close or to accomplish their mission, you will fail most of the time because there will be more variables, other excuses, and blame or forecasting.

No matter what challenges there are, you must be prepared to go beyond what it takes to get the job done. This is huge when it comes to goal achievement. You need to know how much Time, Effort, Insistence, Enthusiasm, and Will Power It takes time to achieve your goals.

Let's think about a time you have trained for your most difficult situation ever?

Did you ever come up short?

Why and what could you have done differently next time?

What is your Financial Goal?

Salespeople lack a proper financial goal which means you will underestimate and undervalue each deal or sale. If you are working for someone and it doesn't achieve your financial goals, you are just completing someone else's financial plan. This is the entire reason wage roles exist, so owners can take advantage of people who don't have a financial goal themselves.

Creating financial freedom is created for you, your family, and your future. Do you want money in the bank? Investments? Travel? Backup? You will never be truly motivated if you don't have a monetary value to closing. Spending is not the problem; all problems are because you have a lack of income. Closing deals and creating an income will fix this. There is no shortage of money in the world and in people's bank accounts. One million dollars is nothing; I bet you have heard so many people say, "O' man, if I had a million dollars, I'd retire."

This is the why you will never have 1 million because it is nothing; if 1 million disappeared from the world economy, nobody would ever know it existed. People are unwilling to complete your financial goal and maybe have false information.

Money doesn't Grow on ....

Well, it does; money can be printed any second.

If you are uncomfortable asking someone for their money, you have the wrong idea. Treat people like millionaires, trust in your product if you believe in your product or services. If you know they are the best, it will improve a customer's situation by either improving their economic position, feeling valuable, or increasing their health safety in life. Then insisting a customer put down a deposit of $5000 or $500,000 something doesn't seem so crazy or pressuring now, does it?

The best salespeople are purpose drivers, charity workers. To fulfil the mission, they have a goal mission purpose, finishing a cycle of action. These charity workers can be masters and committed to the purpose and aligned with the financial goals of the charity.

What is the financial plan for you now?

What is the financial plan for the business as a whole?

What are you all working towards together? Do you even know?

Should you start communicating together as a business?

Do you have Debt to pay?

Do you have investments?

How much income do you want to have in your job?

Money to expand your training in yourself? Do you have a Business Idea?

I don't want anyone here to be afraid of having side businesses and side hustles.

Tell your boss about it, tell your coworkers they need to know so they can help you too.

Your dreams might not be here in this organization, that's ok. No one stays in the same business forever. As a business owner, you should encourage this, encourage growth, and encourage goals here or elsewhere. They will end up staying a lot longer if your business is supportive of you right?

CHAPTER 10
THE RIGHT USE OF LOGIC & EMOTION IN SALES

Sales is a Transfer of Energy

Selling is a transfer of energy that comes from two sources; logic and emotions. Guess what has more influence over a buyer's actions? To explore this further, let's review some of the logical elements that can influence the outcome of a sales call:

- Product knowledge
- Customer knowledge
- Social information
- Sales process
- Diagnostic questions
- Sales-ready messages or call script
- Persuasive proposals
- Persuasive presentations
- Call timing

Most sales training prepares salespeople to tap into the right information, ask customers the right questions, diagnose the right problems, create the right solution, prepare the right proposal, and close the sale at the right time. It all sounds wonderful during the sales-training program, and it looks great on a whiteboard. The trouble is, when salespeople believe that their job consists of building a prefabricated bridge made of the right logical elements from the seller to the buyer, those salespeople will be disappointed 80 percent of the time.

Logic Vs Emotions

Zig Ziglar once said, "Logic makes people think, and emotions make people act." I am convinced that the logic bridge between buyer and seller represents only 20 percent of the buying decision in a B2B setting. If logic was all it took to persuade a buyer, we could move the entire sales process online and eliminate the need for salespeople, just like Amazon did.

What Creates Emotional Impact?

Dr. Albert Mehrabian at UCLA found in his research that feelings and attitudes are communicated 7% by words, 38% by tone of voice, and 55% nonverbally. Since most inside salespeople use the telephone as their main connection with the buyer, how we say what we say (tone of voice) has five times more emotional impact than what we say (the actual words).

What creates emotional impact is the salesperson's ability to do the following:

- Create feelings of trust and rapport.

- Affirm the buyer's need for good self-esteem.

- Sense the buyer's emotions in the moment

- Show empathy.

- Appropriately reflect on the buyer's emotional expressions.

- Adapt to the buyer's rate of speech.

- Harmonize with the buyer's tone of voice.

- Get in synch with the buyer's emotional energy.

- Complement the buyer's moods with uplifting statements.

- Give the buyer emotional space to facilitate free associations.

- Draw out and address the buyer's hidden fears.

- Support and enhance the buyer's positive viewpoints

- Project and maintain positive energy throughout the call.

- Be authentic and spontaneous.

These points describe how sellers need to meet buyers' emotional needs so that buyers become comfortable with sellers. This list is by no means complete, but it creates a composite image that defines likeability.

Sales trainers and sales managers constantly remind us that selling is a people business and that we buy from people we like. Guy Kawasaki tells of how he met Richard Branson in Russia. They met in a green room before a speaking engagement. When Branson asked Kawasaki what airline he used, he learned that Kawasaki was loyal to United because he had the highest status there. Branson didn't use logic to persuade Kawasaki to become a customer; he simply picked up his leg and started to polish his shoes with his jacket. Kawasaki switched to Virgin America in a heartbeat.

It's about time that we recognized that buyers want to deal with likable salespeople, and it's about time that we give them what they want. At our last Sales 2.0-Conference, an attendee told me about her interest in a Sales 2.0 solution that was offered by a sponsor. She said,

"The salesperson in the booth perfectly understood my needs, and I shared our pain points with him in great detail. In the end, he told me that he would put me in touch with his company's rep in my region. That was frustrating since I have to go through the same process all over again."

Isn't it time for buyers to be able to choose the salesperson with whom they want to work?

With new social CRM solutions such as Nimble or Reachable, geographic territories will be giving way to social proximity, in which leads are assigned to salespeople who have the best social connection with prospects.

In the not too distant future, companies will allow customers to select a salesperson who scores highest in likability. Who wouldn't want to get a shoeshine from, Richard Branson or a direct tweet from Zappos CEO Tony Hsieh, or a Facebook "Like" from Michael Dell?

Since most products become commodities faster, the ultimate competitive advantage is the salesperson. In the future, smart companies will give buyers the ability to choose salespeople based on what they believe is the ideal match between professional competence and emotional intelligence. Emotional proximity could be the ultimate competitive advantage.

Optimal Sales Strategy

Have you ever made beer?

Did you know there are only four ingredients: hops, malt, water, and yeast that can make 4 billion recipes. Change one thing, the whole thing changes. Timing, type, where it's grown, how it's grown, all have an effect on the recipe. When you add them together, then they perfect a certain method and then stick with it to get better and better.

The more you practice selling your product, stalls, objections, questions, or anything that comes up, you get better and better. If you're creating a new recipe, it ain't going to be perfect, is it? Just like a business and its service. You need to handle every question.

- Drill

- Practise

- Rehearse

Many objections are similar; If you want to be a master, you need to sell hard. For you to get results, you need to prepare yourself. Watch your,

- Gestures

- Hand Motion

- Tone level

- Responses

Practise with your team members, this builds confidence. Set a time the next week, practise handling these objections. There is a road, a recipe to follow, it's called the road to the sale. We need an exchange of ideas with communication and it is critical in two ways.

If you follow the "The road to the sale", you will increase your sales. This is a step by step recipe to close. This information is vital to gain trust, identify correct products and present proposals, make sense of proposals and how to negotiate the transaction so you get paid.

This is designed to walk you through each step; your success is dependent on knowing and rehearsing offhand, which is memorized for every customer.

Missing any step is like building a house with no walls or cake with no egg. This means you need to believe in the company and believe in what you do. The biggest mistake is that there are no steps and not knowing means broken steps and no confidence in you and in the customer.

Do not be reasonable with this; if you take a shortcut, it slows you down.

Commitments to the road

1. Know the steps off by heart.

2. Know the purpose of each step and benefits.

3. Never skip a step.

4. Always get answers to your questions.

5. Always handle customer's objections, agree to objection.

6. Always be positive (attitude) Can do, will do, yes, I can do that.

7. Always agree

8. Approach each step with service in the back of your mind

CHAPTER 11

BUILD YOUR STEP BY STEP SALES PROCESS

Chapter Overview:

1. Attitude
Manners, feeling, mental state, your expectation, dress, posture, and facial expressions.

2. Greeting
What to say and what not to say, what to expect and how to handle and build rapport to build common ground into the next steps.

3. Fact Finding (Discovery)
What is critical to know is how to communicate to build value for the product or service.

4. Appraisal (Buyer Profile)
This is used when the buyer is trading something in. This sets up the selection and demonstration. So you can structure your transaction.

5. Selection & Demonstration/ Presentation
This vital step identifies products to satisfy wants and needs and buying patterns. Take time to show features and benefits of the products selected that create urgency concern to buy now..

6. Trial Close
Identifies how close the customer is to purchasing.

7. Negotiations

This comes to an agreement, to all parties to agree. Present a proposal and enter negotiations.

8. The Close

Technology and skill to get an exchange of things of value with each other.

9. Delivery

Delivering the product and understanding the customer knows how to use the product.

10. Follow Up

Creatively stay in touch to ensure customers retain to ensure continued satisfaction for repeat and referral. Calls, email, video, personal visits.

Avoid these mistakes during the road:

- Random approaches

- Skipping Steps

- Change order

- Miss or skip a part

- Not getting answers from questions

- Talked out of steps

- Avoid asking questions

- Skip to price

- Unable to handle tough customers

- Too mechanical like a robot

What does Attitude Mean?

Your Attitude Decides who you are:

Your paycheck is dependant on attitude. The reason why this is #1 is because it's critical to your life and the road. Because this is taken before you pick up the phone, get on the phone when you wake up. Before your greet or make a phone call. Without a great attitude, not neutral, not good, BUT GREAT!

It doesn't matter what step you're taking; you need an EXCELLENT attitude. If you have memorized the steps, your attitude will still stop you from the sale. This goes back to being sold on yourself, your company, and to your success. People don't buy from those who they don't feel good around. If they do, they'll decide on something such as price. If you want to have the highest price, you need to have the best and most positive attitude.

You don't need to stand in front of a mirror and say, "I AM GOOD, I AM GREAT, I AM GONNA BE THE BEST." It's just knowing for sure you are going to make the sale in your gut and in your heart. Dress to impress and be a winning professional going after 100billion dollars. Carry yourself like a winner even in the face of adversity. Having great eye contact and smiling even if they have the worst objection. Always smile, and agree, and understand. You want to have service in your heart, nothing to do with money. This first step attitude will determine how far you will go. Hard work will always be hard work if you don't have a good attitude about it.

How do you deliver it?

Communicate positively by saying, "Yes, I will," "excellent, no problem," "I will do anything you want," "I agree with you; I love that idea." Look, you don't have to feel great, but if you don't have a great attitude in your job, you will not succeed. The same product or service is next door. This first step will keep you above the rest.

There are very few people with a positive attitude, you don't realize, but when you stand out by being positive, it shows and is reflected back by the customer. You need to practice this because it's not only your attitude that needs to be positive, but you need to change theirs.

How to stay positive and have a good attitude and keep it?

Your attitude is determined by your thoughts and by the content in your mind, which is affected by the content around you. No different than your body or health by what you put in it. Whatever goes on around your life will be a reflection of your attitude.

How do you stay positive? Control the content in your mind by controlling what you see and hear, what you do and say. If you have positive content put into your mind, you will have those thoughts and speak them.

What have you read and looked at, the content today since you woke up?

Let's open the news? NEGATIVE!
Write your goals down and finish things left undone. Check in with yourself on a scale of 1 to 10. How do you feel right now? You need to have daily meetings to enhance your attitude.

Write a list now of what you are grateful for?

■ Smiling

■ Great attitudes see problems as opportunities Problems = opportunities = money

■ Talking positive

■ Work a plan. Have a plan. A diary task list – Boredom creates problems

■ Wake up early and show up. It makes others feel good too

■ Staying late at work reflects a great attitude; they want to do it; they want to be there.

■ Train consistently. Learn always to learn more

■ Think about solutions, not the problems; what would solve this problem? How can we figure it out? First, look for problems, then focus on the solution.

■ Take high levels of action, regardless of whether you know what you're doing. Keeps you in the zone, which is a scientific place.

■ Stay busy; would you rather be busy than bored?

■ When you're sharing or talking, only talk about the positive and cut negative or gossip. If you have nothing good to say, don't say it at all

■ Don't quit or give up on your goals. Find a better way

■ Refuse to take no for an answer.

■ Read and watch educational content

■ Focus on the potential or future of what people can do, not the past. You can't change the past; you can't change what you cannot control.

■ Be focused on goals, not work focused.

■ Don't complain. It doesn't solve problems, explain the problem and try to come up with a solution. No one wants to hear this, whether you're sick or losing. Do something about it instead.

■ Be grateful and find something to be grateful about. We all have our arms, heads and are alive!

■ Motivate others, push everyone to be positive, train and work. Don't assume the worst or have the worst intentions for people. Always assume they have the best intentions. Regardless of whether they are out to get you.

■ Seek challenges, problems, and situations; the more interested you become, and it gets exciting.

The best sale is the one you make for yourself. Are you sold on:

- Product?
- The Company you work for?
- Yourself?

Why? Write down why you believe in your service? Do you believe in the company? Why? How do you go the extra mile, and what do you do differently than others?

If you don't want to be excellent or great at what you do, then you or even your boss may need to have another think about what you're doing here. As hard as that may be, a business cannot survive if you aren't invested in the company or the business. Toxic people bring companies down.

Positive communication

Let's assume the customer says, "I don't have any money."

What do you say to that?

1. Great attitude
"I'd be happy to do that; of course, we can."

2. Offering all information
Give them other options, give them a million options information overload

3. Have a sense of humor
Let's say a customer says, "I do not want to do it today, no I think I will think about it?" the answer to that, "Great, that's perfectly fine, I hate paperwork, when did you want us to get this started for you?"

4. Understand the customer or know them
"I need to look at other quotes."
"That is smart; we recommend everyone to understand the market. Have you received any thus far? No worries, XYZ and ZX are some other places you can go to." "The differences though X & Y did you want me

to pass on their numbers, or you are happy to stay with us?"

5. Confidence in your service or product
"I don't want to put money down today" What do you say?
"Done, no problem, we don't have to! Sounds great."

6. No problem attitude
"We can't come in," "no worries, I'll come to you."

7. Reassuring the customer
"Can you have this done by Friday?"

What do you say?

"No problem, I will try to do everything to get it done by then."

Here's another example.

"Hey, do you have a penthouse suite available tomorrow night?" You know you're booked out for a month, but you have normal rooms. "Hey, no problem, I'll have a look for you now. If I can't get you into our penthouse, how does the upgraded king suite sound, and if I can upgrade you before tomorrow, I will; how does that sound?"

What have we done there?

Used a positive attitude to change inventory and still solved the customer's problem without losing a customer. Don't worry about customers' problems; that's what you want, always give them the best option that you have without presenting it negatively.

"This is too expensive; I cannot pay this much?"

"Yes, ok, I will see what I can do; if I can't figure it out, I'll make sure someone else here will. I'll get back to you today."

The Greeting

The first moments can never be changed, you have to do this well

To address with kind wishes upon meeting or arrival.

1) Make people feel welcome
2) Introduce yourself
3) Put buyer at ease
4) Get on common ground
5) Differentiate yourself
6) Buyer to turn control to you

Lovely to meet you, my name is...
That's the easy part; control is essential to selling. Ask a manager or director if they can run a business without control.

Are you in control of the conversation, phone call meeting?

Control comes from working the steps.

Control means close.

There are rules:

Always go to the buyer, or always call them. Put your hand out and walk to them.

They are there for themselves, not for you; you need to be interested in them. Whether they came to you, the little thing you can do is walk and go over to them. Treat all like buyers are customers; always assume someone is an opportunity. There is no exception.

Don't look for why they are not buyers, Look for ways you know they could be buyers. Make eye contact and be present with the customer. Listen and remember the name; say it five times in your head. Ask them their name or say their name.

Don't be offended if someone brushes you off or anything. Always smile, shake hands, and be firm. Always say your name or wear a name badge if you can.

How do you put people at ease when you meet them? Unless you don't meet them everyday, they will always be uncomfortable. You need to make sure they are not guarded. You will not get on common ground, turn control or build trust or confidence. People are guarded when they meet new people. You go to a party or do anything new you are not comfortable with.

The more guarded a customer is, it indicates they are more of a buyer. Therefore, it is not a bad thing. You're going to get objections right off the bat when you meet someone. These first objections are reactionary defense responses but are not really objections. Just automatic and are designed just to put the guard up. Don't take it personally; it means nothing for these first defensive reactions.

Agree and acknowledge it, understand and predict it. You are in the people business, not any other industry. The customer won't tell the truth; it doesn't have anything to do with you. However, you need to be responsible because you want to solve this problem. If you show interest, people think it'll take too long; they are pressuring me. People feel obligated if you show interest. You'll even have family members feel obligated to buy something from you hence why they may not come in. Many people come into a store and want to go as quickly as possible.

Buyers Fears

1. Decision making is harder than the money
2. Getting ripped off
3. Financial Insecurity
4. Pressure No one likes pressure
5. Time – It's gonna take too long
6. Obligation
7. Can't say No

Make people feel comfortable

1. Warm greeting
2. Introduce them to the family
3. Handle Fears
4. Address their fears – My job is so you make an intelligent decision and you don't have to make a decision today and my job is to service you.

Fact Finding & Appraisal: Buyer Profiling

Common ground (Be Relatable) Rapport

It is the basis of mutual interest or agreement. The keyword is agreement. You can not get on common ground without an agreement. Forget the idea that opposites attract. It is "garbage"; they always divorce, and in selling, opposites never attract. You need to take the time to get on common ground without taking time to do so.

Most salespeople go out of their way to be on common ground, "O" what do you do for a living? How many kids do you have? etc." Common boring rapport questions. Be authentic and genuine, and what do you have in common with everyone? Common is what we can agree on; we all have blood running through us. They want the information, and you have it; they want in and out, and so do you.

Buyers,

1. Want information; you have it
2. Want to get in and out
3. Make a good decision and you want them to make one
4. They don't want the pressure
5. Money prices, rates and value payment plans
6. Don't want to waste time and you don't want to either

So let's come up with an introduction now that has 3 of these.

"My job today is to make sure you get all the information you need so you have the right service; the decision making is up to you, and let's get it down asap, so we don't waste each other's time."

Information is the Common Ground:

You are in the information selling age to assist and gain control of your customers to improve results. What does every customer you meet have in common? It's information! People avoid salespeople like you; they are coming for information most times. Most sales processes break down because the organization doesn't want to give out information.

Information is the ultimate common ground; you can't just give information. You need to close the deal with it. Use the offer of information separate from giving information. Most salespeople fail because they don't get to the information stage. You don't want to give information before you select the product; they need to be sold on by the company and the product before you give them the information. Use information as the hook.

Fact Finding & Discovery:

Now, what can I get any info on anything before starting? Use surprise in your process, break the cycle of the same old sales routine. So now open with a question: what kind of information are you after today?

The giving of information will be in the end proposal or close. Now to transition into the discovery or fact finding part. Use the offering of information but don't give it. Information gets you information, so the transition to the information stage or discovery stage has been transitioned by asking and offering information.

Thus, when the customer responds with, "I just want a price," you reply back, "Yes definitely, that's what I am here for." Then move on to the next question, in the discovery phase.

This agreement and transition give common ground; if you say anything that is a no or confrontational, it stops the flow and the road to sales. Because we are in the age of transparency and information, you need to transition your business into this way. Economies and customers change, so you need to adopt these changes and information because competition is everywhere. The salesperson must offer the most service and have the most information to close.

Asking customers the right questions:

So most of the defensive reaction responses and questions customers initially ask you might not even be relevant or even what the customer wants, so it's up to you to figure it out.

Questions control the sale; it's impossible to control the sale until you have questions. You might call this qualifying, understanding wants and needs or discovery. It sets up the:

1. Presentation of the product
2. Negotiations
3. How you close the sale

You don't want just to start talking about the products until you know what they want, why, how, and how you can make sense of them making a decision. You can hear people talking about the products and never really understand the right solution for the customer. Why that product? You need to get the answer to that question, why now? Why today?

What brings you here today?

What do you like about what you have?

What would you change?

What would you like to accomplish?

There is a dominant buying motive or triggers.

Here in the 21st century, these questions are important. Some of the biggest mistakes in qualifying are

1) Not asking
2) Ask and not getting the answer
3) Not asking relevant questions that don't make sense
4) Questions that could offend, such as "Am I going to waste my time? Are you buying today? When are you looking to make a decision?"

Because customers are guarded and probably believe in the past, they have been manipulated before. That first thing, attitude is critical, by giving service to help everyone. How can you help your customer so they can answer questions?

This should make you different from the competition.

The "What," the "Why," and the "How." We want to solve a problem, and our goal is to find out what goal your customer has. By determining the what, the why, and the how? What the right product is, why the product suits the customer and how to present the solution.

A guy walks into a phone store and says I want this phone here and points to it. You say, "Great, we can get you that phone. What is it about this phone that you want it?" Don't assume this is the best product for that customer; it may definitely not be.

You are the expert, you are providing the right solutions for the customer, but you need to know why the customer wants that specific phone to then sell him on it and our company. Don't be an order taker; you want to know the what, why, and how.

"So, Mr. Customer, what's the most important thing to you on your next phone?" He says, "The video recording."

"Why is video recording important to you?" He says, "Because of my businesses, I need to record testimonials."

What is the most important thing when you are considering XY?

What about the ---------

What about the ---------

Why is ----------important?

I'll give you an example

Guy wants to buy a house on the gold coast. "Great, Mr. Buyer, what is the most important thing when you're considering buying your next home?" ·

"I want it to be on the gold coast."

"Great, what about the Gold coast do you like?"

"Well, I love the beach."

"Why do you like that?"

"Because I am a pro surfer?"

"So, what else about the Gold Coast is important to you?"

"Well, I have kids, and I want them to go to Burleigh high?"

"O' wow! why Burleigh?"

"Because it has a good reputation."

"Great."

So, now we know that the customer doesn't just want a home on the gold coast; they want a lifestyle that allows them to do what they want and put their kids in a good school. They have kids, how many, etc. you with me?

The what the why the how gets you the way or the road to the sale.

To the Guy with his phone, you say, ok, here's the agreement, (see how I said agreement instead of contract). Words like this affect people as well. I'll get onto these further during closing but signature, what's a better word? Autograph.

So this guy says, nah I don't want to make any contracts, and you say that's great you don't have to do anything today when you want to get started on the video conferencing and get those testimonials together to really boost your business look how great this camera delivers, can you see yourself using it? This phone will pay for itself in no time. How long are you going to be doing your job? O forever, well guess what this is only for 24 months. Understanding this, why see how powerful that is.

Don't put the customer on a product or solution they don't want or need. 50% of all the people who see you want information on a product they will never buy. Have you ever tried buying something and been unsure or uncertain of what to buy?

Give me some examples.

Now how can you take an interest in the needs of what you wanted? What questions can you ask?

Fact Finding:

What problem were you actually trying to find? Create your own economy by taking an interest in people's needs. When you ask or fact find with customers, you can add value, create additional options they may never have thought they needed. You can speed up the process by asking specific and known questions. When you go to the store to buy a roast, what problem are you actually trying to solve? Have dinner, right?

Now, if you asked the question of how many people are going to be there, you might increase the size of the roast you can sell.

Your job is not to change a customer's mind but to find the right product for the right solutions. When you take the time to ask questions, you seem interested, and you will understand the customer when you ask good questions.

1. What would you like if money wasn't an option?

2. Whatdo you want to have that you're not willing to give up?

3. What have you done before that you would like again?

4. What would you like to have next time that you don't have now?

Just like a detective always returns to the scene of the crime to find clues. Any sales cycle, you can go back to a previous sale as to what they will do and want in the future. Tell me about the last phone you bought? Where did you buy it and why did you like it? What's something that you want that you never had before?

Even if they are not getting rid of the last phone or car, still ask and seek clues and want to know about how you can build value from the greeting, fact finding, or discovery.

Let's come up with 22 questions about the X industry.

Examples

Do you want an upgrade or downgrade?

Who will be involved?

How do you want it packaged or delivered?

What other options do you want?

What do you demand that your previous one doesn't?

What major and second benefit do you want?

Why is this product important now?

Why today?

Why now?

Have you ever owned this before?

What are you doing now to solve this problem?

What do you dislike about the thing you are using now?

When is your next payment?

How much did you negotiate?

Did you buy new or old or lease?

How long have you had it?

What was the price?

Would you purchase it again?

Yes, why?

No, Why not?

Has it been worth what you paid for?

Have you made any changes to it?

Now you need to rehearse these questions or have a pad near you. Practice, Drill, Rehearse.

Selection

This section is about what product to show and to demonstrate urgency to have the product and to build value over the value of their money. You cannot convince someone to buy your product unless the value exceeds the value of their money. If the product doesn't solve problems or no love or no confidence, it won't close

1. Selecting
2. Demonstrating

These are two separate things and will make a difference. Knowing each of these will ultimately change how successful you will be.

Selecting the right product is vital, and targeting what product to show, based on what they see and what they have told you to make a decision. This is based on previous fact finding because if they knew what they wanted, for sure, they would have already bought it. No matter how crystal clear the client knows what they want. They would already own it.

In any selling situation, I assume that the client is only closed on what they want and never completely clear on why they want it. From personal experience, 50% of the time, the client is interested in products they don't want or even need, and they'll buy something else.

You will not close on a deal if they are not clear on why they want the product if they don't know why for sure they won't buy. The first rule, no matter how sure they are, they would already have it. Always know you need to clarify for sure you need to fact find.

A great way to find out whether a product is right for a customer is to show them alternate solutions. You want to offer an alternative in EVERY selling situation.

Have you been doing that?.

What is an alternative to what products or services you have right now? Let's try.

In your fact-finding, use an alternate to,

1. Validate and confirm
2. How the customer I want the right solution for them
3. Offer to save money

By offering choices, you show you care and to be sure they are on the right solution. Let's come up with some questions now. How can you present alternate solutions?

Now what this does is that it gives customers information, and the more information, the more they understand and are confident in their decision.

This gives you more information in fact-finding.

How can you offer alternatives?

Would you consider

1. Less
2. More
3. Older or Newer?

Alternates:

1. Help the customer make a decision
2. Help you close more
3. Justify the proposal

It doesn't manipulate or confuse as you might think. You can use this in the close or negotiations; when we spoke before, you said you wanted this. 50% of the time, customers want the wrong product, either too much value or too little value.

Don't be an order taker. Initiate, predict and differentiate. Choices don't confuse people; it allows the mind to make a clearer decision. Always offer alternatives before presenting and before negotiations. This is what you probably have heard most about sales.

How long do I present, what to show and how to tailor it to show?

- The origin story of the product
- Functionality, including features and benefits
- The target market
- The product value for customers
- The key business cases
- Competitor landscape

For a long time, salespeople have been told to sell benefits as opposed to features. But understanding the difference between features, advantages, and benefits is more important as they can all be used to provide value and emotional significance to prospects.

Features:

Features describe the attributes of a product or service. Consider it "the what" the consumer is getting.

Advantages:

Advantages describe the factual significance of the feature. Consider it "the how" it provides value to the consumer.

Benefits:

Benefits describe why the advantage is valuable in a way that emotionally connects with the consumer. Consider it "the why" that value matters for the consumer.

Feature vs benefit:

Features are technical, describing what the product or service does. Benefits, on the other hand paint a picture of the success.

Advantages explain the significance of a feature and how it solves a problem, often in a factual, concrete, or measurable way. Benefits, on the other hand, is subjective and appeal to the emotions or pains of the prospect.

Salespeople commonly sell features to show they are getting their money's worth, but it doesn't equate to more value.

When you throw the kitchen sink, two things happen. Firstly, they feel like they are salesy and they don't understand the situation.

Secondly, the salesperson may not hit on the impactful value that truly matters to the prospect.

To be a successful salesperson, sell benefits and leave out info that may not pertain to the prospect.

No one will buy unless they can see the benefit in their lives and a clear view of it.

So what are some examples?

Here is an example of a Tesla,

Feature:
Electric

How:
Can using electric battery energy as apposed to fuel energy

Why:
To save you money and the environment for your children s future

Can you come up with more?

Draw a three column table to do it for your product or service?

You can make mistakes with product knowledge

1. Don't know enough
2. Share too much information
3. Don't know about competition

Become an expert on everything about your company and services. Know how your product is different from your competitor's. What products does your competitor have? Never talk negatively about competition.

You need to build value on your features, advantages, and benefits. If your products are the same with competition, you are the only difference.

How much do you know about your products or services?

What are all your current products or services?

What do your competitors offer?

The greatest advantage you have is not your product; it is a fact that your competitor will not be prepared and have the same knowledge as you do.

Personalize the Presentation.

The "Why?"

The biggest question is what does the customer want and why?

Your job is to find out. And what they will pay today.

The Motive?

Means or desires that cause a person to act.

You should always be crystal clear on this to cause the person to do something. So what is their motivation? When you close something, you are giving them something, and they are giving you something.

Why do people buy?

- Appearance
- Performance
- Economical
- Security and safety

These are the only reasons people buy things. What of these does your client want?

Let's write a list of how your product or service can improve the above. Which ones wouldn't it fill? Why? It doesn't have to fit all, but it does have to fit some, and you have to have a reason.

What's the biggest thing you have purchased? What category did it fill most? And how did it do that?

Before you move into the presentation, you need to reassure the customer I am going to get you a price and all the information you will need to make an informative decision and get permission to present.

You want control of this part of the presentation, do not let anyone else present the product or service to you. Because they will shortcut it, so maintain control of this part and ask would you allow me to show you the reason why our customers give us 5-star reviews, and we continue to operate at such high standards. Would you allow me to present the features, advantages, and benefits to you?

Let me know this.

If you think that's great, let me show you. This is where you want to go into detail about your proposal or product; it has to be the specific product or service initially. Now, what product have we selected?

Let's now move into explaining every single FAB you can. You need

• Full attention.
• Only have the single product as a solution.
• Try to have a copy or have the customer have the proposal or car in front of them.

Break it down into parts, 4-6 maximum parts.

So let's do 6 parts. How can you break down the chosen product or service you have into 6 parts?

Let's do it with a Tesla

1) Inside
2) Front
3) Passenger sides
4) Back
5) Drivers Side
6) Driver seat

So you need to find out what is the most important part, so for someone maybe the inside or the back is the most important.

Once again, ask your customer whether you can explain the presentation and tell them you are going to start on the inside and go over x y and come back to the inside, ok. Stop me at any time.

Always make sure you say stop at any time, and reassure the customer if he has any price objections. "I'll make the price right for you, don't worry, if I were unable to make you happy with the price, then I would have done a bad job."

price objections. "I'll make the price right for you, don't worry, if I were unable to make you happy with the price, then I would have done a bad job."

No matter what the product or service is, you need to drive it, much like a car salesman. You drive the proposal, go through it. Give a demo presentation.

Always

■ Get permission

■ Give a time frame

■ Invite questions

■ Start in the same place and know where you want to go

■ Reassure the customer

Rules of the demonstration

■ Goal

■ Show improved value or efficiency

■ You need to be there and be with the customer.

What are the Dominant Buying motives again?

■ Appearance
■ Performance
■ Economy
■ Security
■ Safety

So before presenting a solution, make sure

1. You are in control.

2. You are sure about the product/service

3. You are giving the presentation

4. You ask the customer to stop at any time

5. Slow down and maintain attention of your customer

6. The customer is comfortable.

7. The presentation is known and you know
if offhand

During the presentation

1. Be assumptive with the solution to them

2. Reassure price concerns

3. Be obsessive and be engaging

4. Assure or retrieve any information

Assumptiveness or language

Putting the customer in fit or projecting ownership or the service or product into the future. Be confident when presenting and create mental ownership by assuming.

Positive assumptions and negative assumptions; never use negative assumptions. Always assume only the best in people and the best solution. Asking questions during the presentation such as,

"Will the car fit in your garage?"

The performance of your car is important, isn't it?

Who else is going to be impressed with your new....?

Come up with some assumptive questions now for your product or service.

We can still fact find during the presentation.

Who else will be driving your car?

Mental ownership precedes every purchase, no matter how small or large. If you're going to get something, you own it in your mind before you bought it.

Customers object to the presentation, "I don't have time, I don't need what I already know, I just want the price." You need to know how to handle these because you need to build value regardless of what they say.

Most objections are just reactionary, so first you agree.

"I Don't need to see how it works."

Reply, "I didn't ask you to see how it works; I agree; I don't want to show you how it works; I just want to show you some unexplained or maybe some unknown details about the product or service.

"I know this is what I want."

"I understand and would not allow you to do business if you were not educated about what you're getting for your money."

"I don't have time."

"I understand your time is valuable, and we don't want to waste each other's time if you could allow me the courtesy of 5 minutes to show you these things."

"If you think it's a waste of time, I'll eat my own hat if you don't enjoy the next 5 minutes."

Be committed to explaining your proposal or presentation and go over the top and all the way because you need to build your confidence and the confidence in your customer with the entire presentation.

You need to be able to sell yourself, your product, and the company. Take the time to sell everything, not just the product. Whatever it is, maintenance, landscaping, lawyers, everything can be shopped. YOU cannot be shopped. So you have to sell.

1)   YOU

2)   Company

3)   Product

Let's come up with a FAB now. What does your company do differently? Now, what about you? What FABs do you have?

Confidence, Professionalism, commitment, follow up, persistence, customer satisfaction, service.

So here's an example

Mate, we can use x and y down the road.

I hear you man, let's assume you can. But now you don't get me, and I don't come with the deal. You've met them, and you know this company, and you wouldn't be sitting with me if you weren't confident in what they had to offer. So let's do this.

You want to dominate this market and be happy with the business and company, who you work for, and your products.

The price or resistance to price is based on your presentation; no other phase has more other effects than this.

How do you do this? Go overboard, be obsessed and passionate. Get full attention; you got to want to love attention and be an entertainer. It is just standard to be desensitized by images and content. You need to get people's engagement.

1)   Make huge claims that no other competitor can get

2)   Get them involved, touch feelings, and check lines or parts in the proposal.

We've said it before, and we're going to say it again: features don't sell, benefits do.

Your product might have the fastest part on the planet, or your service might rank number one in the Totally Amazing awards, but none of that means a thing to your potential customers.

Customers don't care what you have or what you've done. Like everyone else, they're only really interested in stories – most often their own. As such, you should learn how to write the right narratives.

Stories sell:

Keith Queensbury of Johns Hopkins conducted an analysis of 108 Super Bowl adverts. He found that,

"Regardless of the content of the ad, the structure of that content predicted its success."

In other words, telling a story was better than listing features (or anything else for that matter).

Freytag's pyramid

'Freytag's pyramid.' Licensed under Public domain via Wikimedia Commons.

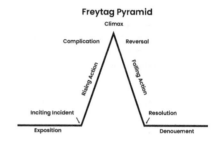

The more complete the story being told in the ad, the more successful the ad. In fact, the more of the five elements of the traditional dramatic structure, shown in Freytag's pyramid that was included, the better the ad did.

This five-act storytelling structure dates back to Aristotle and is exemplified in Shakespeare's plays. It might not be new, but it remains as effective as ever.

So, well-told stories sell, but why? As Harrison Monarch argues in the HBR, 'A story can go where quantitative analysis is denied admission: our hearts. Data can persuade people, but it doesn't inspire them to act.'

Storyteller's secret

Human beings are natural storytellers. We instinctively build a narrative: whether it's of our lives, what's happening outside our window, or even the dramatic encounters of geometric shapes on a screen. As Frank Rose explains:

"Just as the brain detects patterns in the visual forms of nature — a face, a figure, a flower — and in sound, so too it detects patterns in information. Stories are recognizable patterns, and in those patterns we find meaning." (15)

Not only do stories help us link points of information together and create cause and effect explanations of the world around us, but they also trigger something important in our experience.

'The brain, it seems, does not make much of a distinction between reading about an experience and encountering it in real life; in each case, the same neurological regions are stimulated,' says Annie Murphy Paul. When someone describes kicking a ball, our motor cortex lights up. When someone describes a singer as having a 'velvety voice,' our sensory cortex lights up. And so on. (16)

So when we listen to a bunch of bullet points, we hear a load of language. When we listen to a story, we live it.

Selling your selling points with stories

So a story lights up our brain and inspires us to action. How does that link to sales? Well, there's a little more to the story...as it were. Research at Princeton, led by Uri Hasson, has found that the brains of a person telling a story and a person listening to that story can synchronize:

When the woman spoke English, the volunteers understood her story, and their brains synchronized. When she had activity in her insula, an emotional brain region, the listeners did too. When her frontal cortex lit up, so did theirs. The woman could plant ideas, thoughts, and emotions into the listeners' brains by simply telling a story.

Alongside this ability to influence is the fact that people automatically link stories to their own experiences in order to make them more relatable.

This means you can build your selling points into a story that tells the tale of frustration or problem that the listener can associate with their own experience. You can then 'plant' your business as the happy resolution to that story. Once you've planted that idea, the listener will continue with the narrative of their own experience and 'come up' with the idea of using your product or service to solve their issue.

Even better, if you tell your story with positive sensory descriptions, your selling points will elicit those positive experiences for your listeners.

So rather than:

"My widget speeds up data processing by 20 percent,"

You say,

"I was struggling for time, constantly running and feeling the pressure of clients demanding data. I simply wasn't ready. So I decided to do something about it. I developed this widget, which processes the data 20 percent faster, and all of a sudden, I had time to breathe, and my clients were praising me rather than hounding me."

You need more than a good yarn

What makes a good story, great though? Is just telling a story enough? Why do some stories catch our collective attention while others make us shrug with indifference?

"Good stories are strange...Good stories are startling...The narrative excitement of the great scientific theories, far from residing in their reassuring simplicity, lies in their similarly radical exclusions, their shocks," argues Adam Gopnik of the New Yorker.

And as the Super Bowl ads and Shakespeare prove, you also need your five acts (as shown above). Don't ruin the story by skipping directly to the happy ending: good stories require controlled suspense. That's what keeps us engaged.

Add Personas to Your stories

Personas have come up quite a lot on Bad Language lately and with good reason. They're really important for figuring out not just who your audience is, but what exactly it is they want to hear.

When you pitch your product, you have to make it seem like weaving it into every reader's personal story. Trying to appeal to everyone with a general story, however, will resonate with no one. Personas let you be specific to an audience: general to a particular group, as it were.

Personas help you hone in on the problems your typical customers face and common objections they throw up. They also tell you a little about their likes and dislikes, lifestyles, and personalities. This gives you a clue as to how to shock and startle and what tensions will resonate best with the people most likely to buy from you.

Storytelling is eternally effective; but how we tell stories changes.

Research suggests that overused phrases don't light up any part of the brain other than the language processor, even if they contain an action or feeling. They use the example of having 'a rough day,' however, there are plenty of other clichés and stock metaphors out there that you should avoid.

Keep your storytelling fresh: and as you tell the tale of your selling points, make your audience feel as though they are biting into a juicy, tart raspberry rather than munching on some stale, flat pancakes.

Trial Closing

Trail closing is a test, not a jury trial. But we want to focus on the end of the presentation. It allows you to tell what the customer is thinking and an attempt to close the sale before closing

Trial closes are very important

- Provide value

- Low risk

- Asking for an opinion and not closing for a decision.

It's a measurement, not a full commitment and shows you where you can adjust for the close.

Example: Trial Close

• On a scale of 1 to 10, how do you rate this?

• If there are no other questions, can you please put your name here?

Get new data and discern whether they are 100% on the right product and are they on it?

Some other trial closes you can use.

• It looks like you like this, do you?

• Do you prefer the larger or smaller one?

• What are you going to do first?

These are assumptive and putting ownership.

• Are you even ready to close, does the customer?

• What will you do with it?

• Anyone else?

• Can you see yourself winning this?

• What other benefits would you like to see?

• What ones are you going to use and why?

Trial closes can be put anywhere. I've been saying a lot already.

- What do you like so far?

- Do you have enough information to make a decision?

- Is there anything you want to add or change?

- Anything you don't see value in?

When you write up you still want to keep asking trial closes

- Whose name will this be under; do you have any partners?

- Did you want to put it in your company's name or yours?

- Is there any reason you wouldn't want to do this?

- What is your billing address?

Push to make dreams come true. If you don't push others to invest in you, your dreams won't come true, and you will be pushing for others. Don't worry about the price or what you think you or the customer can afford, remember to treat them like millionaires. It's the problem you're solving.

Objections to Trial Closes

What problem were you actually trying to find? Create your own economy by taking an interest in people's needs. When you ask or fact-find with customers, you can add value and create additional options they may never have thought they needed. You need to start using these "closes," and 100% you will have people say heaps of objections. When you hear objections, don't be disappointed or frustrated, it's good because you're moving forward on the answer. Work through every scenario. Roleplay trial, close objection handle.

With the ten trial closes, let's come up with objections you may hear and put a handle on each one.

Customers don't just buy the product; they think, who's going to take care of me after? The more complicated the product, the bigger the customer service it needs. Who's going to be there when you're not? This is included in your FAB. No matter what you're

selling, you need service before, during, and after the sale.

Companies quit serving people, there's so much competition, and people want service, and we have been focused on getting the cheapest product for the easiest convenience, i.e., online. Customers have forgotten about the additional service you can give by talking to them. Show your customer around the business. Ask them if they have met the receptionist, the owner, or others in the business.

Show them the service base and give them the FAB of the company, then explain what happens next. That is the best way to assume ownership of the sale. Selling them the company again with the ease of the next steps.

What are your business's next steps when signing the deal or after? Make them feel like the company is a family or the business is a family.

The write up or details for your proposal or quote

Some might think the "write-up" means you get it, you win, you sold. But it isn't "close." It gets the customer to sit down and come up with the proposal. I am writing to everyone. Average 40% of customers are written up into a proposal. If you make a proposal for everyone 100% and close 0%, that's worse than writing up 10% of customers and closing 100 of them.

Why do we write people up even if they are not ready? You have nothing to lose when you do this. They might change their minds. If you put too many conditions, you remove people. Write them with no conditions. Control the selling process by being prepared on the road of the sale. You don't lose it because you present someone with numbers. If you work for someone, then you need management approval for this.

Some excuses why people don't close

1)   Buyer won't commit, why write them up?
2)   Owes too much many can't afford it
3)   Don't think buyer can get financing
4)   They won't pay enough
5)   Not with decision maker
6)   Buyer doesn't have enough time
7)   Buyer doesn't have all the bits and pieces of info to make the deal

Even with any of these, still write a proposal or do a quote for them"

What things that need to happen before you write up someone

1.   Attitude
2.   Great Presentation
3.   Peace of mind
4.   Commit to writing everyone up a proposal
5.   Team work

Write-ups are putting details down to proposals. You need to put people through this step and swing the bat to get them through. Examples of moving to this step could be

"Let's go inside," and

"Let's go through the numbers" or

"Let's go through the key numbers."

The customer may say,

"I need to think about it."

Your response to that should be,

"Perfect, I want you to think about it. I want to give you all the information so you can make an informative decision."

"I take full responsibility for your decision."

The customers may also say,

"We're not buying till...."

Your Response, "No problem, let's give you an idea of what it will cost anyway."

They may say, "I need my partner."

Your Response, "Great, that's fine. I wouldn't want you to make a decision without them. I am just going to put the details together so you can have all the information for them. let's go."

Another one, "I can't get financing."

Your response, "I guarantee this won't affect it, I will ensure you get financing."

They may say, "I gotta sort my finances out first."

Your Response, "Perfect, I'll just write up all the information first so you can give them to your finance company."

Negotiating
& Closing the deal

The goal of this is to be a master at closing the sale so you can get what you want in life and in your career. The close separates those that have from those who don't. All the hard work you have done with a client or customer all comes down to the close.

Life is all about negotiating; this isn't just sales; it applies to everyone. Nothing truly happens until you get the support and close someone and something. It differentiates the dreamer from the dreams coming true. If you can close funding for your dreams, you can make those dreams a reality. You need skill and ability as is needed by everyone to get what you want in life and in your career. Bill Gates, Steve Jobs closed everyone on their ideas. You know these people had abilities.

The cost of Not Closing:

There is no cost greater than the inability to close someone on your products, services, or dreams. Your money, energy, and resources to get a customer interested and then not closing are expensive. Your belief and self-confidence are lost. You don't want to do your job. You could spend 2 hours on a transaction or two years. You had them at the negotiation table but didn't close.   What happened?

Everything has to start over, follow up and get them back into the cycle. It's unfinished. How do you feel when you have something unfinished? You want closure to finish a cycle. It also doesn't help your customer; they need your product or solution so that they don't lose as well. Everyone loses; even the economy loses when you don't close.

The critical exchange point at which you close.

There is no cost greater than the inability to close someone on your products, services, or dreams. Your money, energy, There is a transfer point to get the customer to take action so that you exchange something they have for something you have. This specific moment where you acquire an agreement, and both parties take action or actions then things of value are exchanged if nothing exchanges there are no closes.

So you need

1) Action
2) Exchange of value

For the first time in negotiations, you need to really benefit your prospect; until this exchange takes place, you can't be of service because you haven't closed. You haven't really created value. Most people are stuck in the sales process. This failure to close on a critical exchange point leads to the failure of a complete economy.

Most people don't ask for the close because they don't truly understand what the close is. The world turns, and the money is exchanged due to a close. If there were no closes, there would be no economy.

Create your future by determining the amount you close.

How do you start to persist, handle objections and emotions, and get to that critical exchange point?

The winners' exchange means if what they received is what you have given, you will be able to repeat the process. The person needs to feel like a win and go do this and repeat this because the perceived value was greater than the value given.

Promise free shipping. Price was not the problem; it was the cost of shipping. So, ASOS and black milk clothing do this well; it's all free returns. Let's understand this further.
Give someone a bottle of water for, say, $5 and ask them not to drink it. Do you think you closed? No, you sold them, but you didn't close them. If you don't follow up, you haven't closed. You want someone to drink the water so that they can tell others about the water and feel they have received the value worth their money. Have you ever had buyer's remorse after they have bought something? That's exactly the kind of thing you need to avoid.

How can you give customers more now that they think it's more than what it's worth?

Let's look at your products or services. Do you believe this value is worth it? Why? If you haven't yet had someone buy from you, you want referral promotions and reviews.

How can you get someone to love what you have done? Do we have customer reviews set up? Do we have referral systems in place?

The ultimate goal is to finish the transaction to close the door. Close the door to the sale. Get the prospect to take action where the transaction is complete, and you both walk through a door and close it behind you. The goal is not to continue negotiating; the goal is to finish.

Simple closes

"Let's do this."

"Let's get the ball rolling."

"Can I get your autograph?"

"Will it be cash or card?"

"I understand. Let's do it anyway."

"Let's make a decision now."

Closing and selling are completely different.

How do you know how to close and repeat that again and again? If you don't know, you will never be able to predict things in future sales. If you know what's going to happen in the future, you can predict stuff, right? You quit making excuses and accept that it's all because of you. Many people like to take the credit when you close but not when you don't close the deal.

Knowledge comes from knowing how it happened, what caused it to happen and what will happen in the future, and what you need to do in the future to make sure. Everyone can close a deal, but can you repeat it over and over at high rates? You need to know the game; you don't want to believe in luck or chance.

Like we spoke about knowledge before and knowing responses and when someone is buying. If you don't have the knowledge and wisdom, you will get a "NO." Knowledge about the close means you go to work with confidence and happiness.

1) They don't know there is a skill of closing

2) Don't believe it's a numbers game, it isn't luck or random chance.

3) Spend time to master the close in your organization

Now, no college or uni teaches selling. But closing was a step that was to be done at the end of the sales process. Don't ALWAYS BE CLOSING

You may have heard that before. But you can't at the start, can you? Don't assume people around you or who work with you know anything or know how to close. Most salespeople don't know anything about negotiation and closing.

You can learn how to close from experience, which can mean failures and making up all these ideas or the other way is to create an experience using drills, responses, and preparing scripts. Create objections, set up closing situations.

1)   Learn from past experiences

2)   Create experiences, new ones (rehearse and role play)

Let's put some questions together. Where would you put those in the scale?

- Intro
- Discovery
- Presentation
- Negotiation
- Close

Let's start running some role plays. This should happen daily.

- Record yourself and your team and check fault yourself.
- Be tough on each other.

The toughest time is the close. This is when you ask someone to take some sort of action. This make   or breakpoint is when the sales and customer shakes. Freaking out because they don't know what they are doing, these wild reactions doubt themselves, and the mission and the buyer pick it up. The customer gets lost in your negative responses. From your

a)   Lack of understanding
b)   Lack of preparation

Closing is a service to the customer; it's more than just making money. You are aiding someone to make a decision. You want to rehearse these and practice with real people 100 times completely.

You need not be afraid of this. How is it that you enjoy the customer, you, company, and product but then back up when you ask for the close?

Why do sales people fear closing?

1) Outdated approaches
2) Misinformed about the simplicity of sales
3) Fear of being pushy or being offensive or pressuring
4) Fear of rejection
5) Lack of tools, ammo process and many different closes to wrap the deal up

Do you believe your product is superior?

Do you believe your company is superior?

Why not? Give me reasons.

Why wouldn't this be the best solution for the customer, and why wouldn't you ask if you knew it was?

Making closing a service to the customer, helping the customer to make that decision is imperative to both you and the customer. The value of the close is the most important. The relationship by itself will not get you to a close. Most people don't buy from you or the company or presentation; it's the close that closes the deal, right?

Logic Vs Emotions

Agreement is a more friendly term. Don't use "contract." Instead, use

"I agree; I am with you, I understand." It develops a relationship.
The Difference between a Contact and a Contract is "R," which is a relationship. It doesn't matter how much they like you. Likable people attract and agreeing attracts people. Prospects make decisions with help from your closing. People are so highly insecure about money, the ability to create money and make decisions. That's why your service is so valuable to make good, valuable decisions. People will flow money to people they like, and relationships are critical. Don't just be nice, though.

We need deals done; most people put too much significance on being nice, not focused on, "let's go, let's roll, let's do the deal." "Sir, you have been thinking about this for three years, and we have been here for three years." Let's get the deal done.

You need to transition that exchange; the nicest decision is if you make them make the decision. You shouldn't feel bad or feel scared because you have been through the sales process, you have found the right solution, and your solution is the right one. If it weren't for that, you wouldn't be closing. At least handle the objection 3 or 4 times, stalls, or complaints. You need to be persistent to close.

You need to have the ability to come to an end and complete an agreement, not try but complete. This represents about 20% of your time but 100% of your money earned. Put the most amount of time for a successful close because that's where the money is. Build trust, build credibility, and then close. In short, your buyer must be sold on the product and want it, love it, and have confidence in it. The customer must trust you to be credible. You have to be talking to a decision-maker to make a deal. They need to see more value in the product or service than what your exchange is. They have to be financially qualified to make the purchase.

Different ways to get the same thing done or alternate closes:

It's better to get a no than nothing when you never asked. If you do push yourself into the situation, you will find better solutions. Push yourself into the deal knowing you want you to do everything. The price myth is another reason you don't attempt to close. If you do not ask, you will never ever get anything you want.

Most people are unwilling to deal with the emotional discomfort between the exchange. You have to be willing to handle the emotional output to be with others to do deals with people. People get loud, annoyed, or angry. Negotiations, agreements, decisions, and money, people get emotional on these things, but you need to make nothing of it.

Have you had anyone get emotional? How do you handle it?
Let's come up with scenarios where people have become emotional. Now you need to handle this logically. So how can you be logical from the reactions you just listed?

Buyers can get emotional, it's fine, and they are just expressing something. You can remain calm. Stay interested and continue negotiating. Do not react If someone gets angry or feels like you are pressing.

You need to be completely sold on your product or service. You have to have faith deep-seated in order for you to control to gain the close. You need to be closed on the product or service and so convinced that what you have is incredible. You should not allow any other decision because you believe, not because you are pushy or pressuring. That's called passionate persistence. The passion and belief have to be reassessed from time to time.

In every exchange, there is a sale; he who is most passionate or most sold will do the most selling and convincing. If they are sold more on waiting, you're going to get sold by them. There will be an action such as I'll think about it or I have to ask. Close or be closed. The party who is most sold will do the most closing.

For years and years, over the last 50 years in sales, it has taught us to handle objections, right? But most of the time, customers' objections are merely complaints. This has not been clarified enough; you need to distinguish the difference between objections and complaints. After years of research, most objections are simply customers talking and complaining.

Here's a rule, moving forward, treat every objection as a complaint further validated. People always automatically complain about things, life situations, deals, offers, and new things.

Most of the time, you will have to handle a complaint with,

"No worries. I understand."

"O man, the price is too high."

"No worries, man, I understand."

"This is our proposal, and the next steps are a 10% deposit."

"The truth is you know this is a fantastic price for what you want; let's do this cash or card?"

So the steps are,

1) Agree
2) Close
3) Validate later

A prospect might say, "I need to talk to my spouse."

You say, "Let's work this out; your partner knows you're doing this; let's do this today."

Or, "I agree if your partner were anything like mine, they know you'd make the right decision, so let's roll. Did you want a bank deposit or card 10% deposit?"

Another reason people don't close is, you don't have any close to pursuit through the negotiation. People aren't born great or masters at closing or at golf. You just need an arsenal of ammunition to deliver that is natural to deliver to customers. There are hundreds of different types.

Types of closes

1) Money
2) Time
3) Stalls
4) Product and Service
5) Basic Objections

Once you find an objection and not a complaint, which may be the right product, too little product, too much product, not the decision-maker, not with the decision-maker. We need to commit to practice and role-play these within your workplace.

The incorrect barrier may also get you. You might think one thing, but it could be something else. And you may not realize or understand it was the closer and management, the ultimate barrier and only barrier to every closed customer.

What you focus on is what you attract. If you believe credit cards are a problem, if you think that sleeping on it, if you believe that you can't make a valued decision now or you need to think or wait or think about it, that's your belief if you accept that.

The Rules of closing:

These rules are like those in a game; they need to be applied. You won't achieve true success without them.

1) Always be seated when negotiating and closing (present on your feet terms on the seat)

2) Proposals need to be written because talking is cheap. Write it down, validate, verify, always write down what you're saying, disclose everything. It should be used to build positivity.

3) Clearly communicate. Know what you're going to say with confidence and tone

4) Eye Contact

5) Have a pen

6) Use humor

7) Always ask minimum of three times for the sale

8) Have multiple closes available

9) Stay with buyers at all times and guide them through all the next steps, don't leave; if you need to check with someone, text or call the manager for approval there.

Closing Guide

1) If the payments are not agreeable, I wouldn't expect you to go through with it. I am confident that our financial lenders will make your payments agreeable and affordable.

2) I agree it's (What customer said) let's do it anyway, we will take care of you.

3) I agree it's a lot of money. I expect you knew that before you started looking; let's get the ball rolling today, cash or card?

4) I agree (Customer Objection) that's exactly what the last customer said; for us to secure you, will you sign/send the documents back, and we can get it looked after for you.

5) I agree; I bet this isn't the first or the last time you spent more money than you expected. Let us look after you. Will it be cash or card or documents signed?

6) I know it's too expensive, or you have to think, but you should congratulate yourself for even making this sort of decision. Autograph here or pay cash or card?

7) I agree if everything was right, would you make a decision? What is it? Price, Product, or Us? Let us get this sorted for you today.

8) I agree you can wait. You're either going to do it now or later. Let's make you the first, and let's make sure you are looked after now so that you can achieve what you want now instead of later.

9) Of course, you can wait, but I want to get it done today so you can focus on life and enjoy the benefits today, so let's get your autograph here, or how would you like to pay, deposit cash or card?

10) Look, , there is never the best time; you will always have things on. Let's get it done so you can relax and get benefit right now.

11) Look, since I am unable to get you to do it later, what about if you can commit with me sometime in the future? How does that sound?

12) I understand you can wait; this offer I am currently giving you is a now or never offer, so let's do this.

13) The sooner we get this done, the more you are free to get the other things done. So let's do it now so you can get all the other stuff done.

14) When was the last time you surprised your partner? Let's do it.

15) Ok great, so the other person isn't available; they ultimately control the decision, or is it a joint decision? If joint, let's agree to ownership. Delivery and equipment are only subject to a third party. If so, that means write it up today, and that way, it's all subject to a third party, and I know you are committed, and I would be appreciated by that.

16) Sir, thought is instant; think of an Elephant. It's not something that takes time. What we need is a decision, yes or no? If not, then it must be something to do with the understanding of either Price or Product or Company; which is it?

17) I understand that thinking about it won't change the fact that it will save you money, and sooner or later you'll do it so that you can think about more important things like X Y, we can do cash or card, what will it be?

18) As a consumer myself, when I was in this sort of situation, I wasn't on the right product, maybe the finance conditions had not been addressed. What do you think it could be?

19) Yes, I understand the paperwork is important, is there anything specifically in the documents you want to read that you may not have an understanding of yet? If not, let's get it done now, and I can ensure that we go over it now.

20) Certainly, you can wait; what happens while you wait? It will cost you XY, you will still require this, and lastly, nothing changes except you need to make a decision later about it. What do you say? Let's get it done today for you?

21) I understand; I don't like making rash decisions. With what I have gone over, we have spent all this time going through this with you. You wouldn't be making a rash decision because you know what there is in the market now. Let's make the right decision now. Do you believe this is the right decision?

22) I agree you shouldn't make a rash decision; how long have you been thinking about it already? I know you need it; not only would it not be rash, but it would also be right, and you can't afford not to do this. How did you want to do this?

Importance of Reviewing Terms of Agreement:

Always REVIEW contract/agreement terms... no surprises and creating the illusion (or reality) of transparency and straightforwardness.

Ask them how they justify the expense of your service, basically making "rationalize" the person out loud and to themselves in front of you (mental programming)

Always ask/check for influencers and buy-ins & dm's

The Follow Up Strategy

- Fundamentals
- Focus on the top of the funnel
- The impact of making another call
- Lead nurturing beyond the initial conversation
- 9 ways to radically improve your follow up results
- Use a follow up schedule
- Use different contact formats
- Time your follow up for maximum impact
- Leverage email templates
- Track ACTUAL contact attempts
- Always get agreement on next steps
- Use content to expand the range of potential touchpoints
- Track email opens and click throughs
- Use call down lists

Most companies are only focused on closing hot leads. At a first glance, this seems to make sense. Focus on your best opportunities, right? The problem with this approach is that it leaves a lot of good leads that just need more time and nurturing to wither on the vine.

Most companies simply don't realize how many leads are won or lost at the top of the funnel. By specifically focusing on improving your contact rate and your meeting rate, you can easily increase the yield of opportunities from your existing lead flow.

For example, when we improved contact and meeting rates in our sales funnel. We improved upstream contacts and meeting rates. Our closing rates increased by 40%. Directly translated to bottom-line revenue.

Focus on optimizing the initial stages of the sales funnel as much as the latter stages.

The write up or details for your proposal or quote

People don't always pick up on the first try, and sometimes it takes multiple calls to make contact. I've heard every reason under the sun for not making another call, including, "If they were really interested, they would have answered the first time or called me back."

The question is, are you a salesperson or an order taker?

Order takers send documents, accept contracts, and don't concern themselves with anything upstream from those tasks. Salespeople work to make contact, then deal with objections, and finally match problems with solutions to help prospects discover value in their service.

Some agents may genuinely feel that repeated follow-up attempts will only annoy the prospect, but we find this rarely to be the case as long as no more than six calls attempts are made over a period of several weeks. Very few companies meet or exceed this threshold.

So how many calls should you make before giving up?

Below is a contact probability arc created using sales data on persistence. It shows the correlation between making another call and the probability of making contact.

The chart below yields some interesting insights:

Calling three times is 68% more effective than calling once

Calling six times is 94% better than calling once. This same research also reveals that leads contacted after the 6th call are 45% less likely to convert than leads contacted before that point. The good news is that as the odds of making contact go up with each additional call, the odds of agents making another call are also going down.

The field is most crowded at the outset but then thins down considerably, leaving a very wide opportunity for persistent companies. Takeaway: Be persistent in your follow-up. Tenacity pays huge dividends.

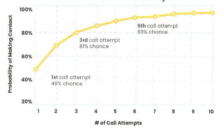

Contact Probability Arc

Lead Nurturing Beyond the Initial Conversation

Not all leads are ready to buy right out of the gate, but that doesn't mean they aren't worth pursuing. If real estate is about location, location, location, lead nurturing is about follow up, follow up, follow up.

The goal is to stay in front of prospects in a way that creates value rather than annoyance. It's part art, part science.

A good lead nurturing effort matches the buying timeline of every prospect, whether that be a week, a month, or a year. The pace and tenor of follow-up may change over time, but it should never just stop because the prospect wasn't ready to buy immediately. The companies that master this can build a long-term asset out of their leads rather than running a churn and burn operation that wastes good leads. Takeaway Learning to nurture long-term leads will radically increase the yield on your existing lead flow.

Now that we've established how important good follow-up is, now it's time to get down to the nuts and bolts of making yours better.

Enter the big list of follow up strategies and tactics

1. Use a Follow up Schedule. Don't leave the follow up to chance.

Most salespeople fail to invest in setting and communicating clear expectations for what good follow-up actually looks like beyond some vague generalities. Get specific. Create a follow-up schedule that outlines when calls and email follow-ups should be happening.

Your team will appreciate that you take it seriously and respond better with clear expectations. The goal is to maintain appropriate, timely follow-up no matter if they're ready to sign a contract today or ask you to call them back in two months.

Starting out, two basic contact schedules should suffice, one for active leads and another for passive leads.

Active leads are responsive and ready to buy in the near term. Passive leads are still qualified but are on a longer-term buying time frame.

Follow-up schedules can and should extend all the way out to 12 months, although the tenure and frequency of communications should change significantly as time goes on and based on the level of interest displayed from the prospect. Takeaway Mapping out your follow-up schedule means no leads fall through the cracks.

2. Use Different Contact Formats

It's as simple as it sounds. Use more than one way to reach out. Email, snail mail, phone, text, social, it's all on the table. The goal is to touch prospects in different ways in order to stay top of mind and stand out from the competition.

Get a hold of people in whatever way works. Think outside the box.

3. Time Your Follow up for Maximum Impact

In business, as in life, timing is everything. Some days of the week and times of the day are simply better for making sure you connect with prospects.

In fact, according to research: (17)

Thursday is 26% better for open email rates than the worst weekday, Monday.

Thursday is 49% better for phone contact rates than the worst weekday, Tuesday.

Takeaway: Not all days of the week or times of day are created equal. Try to time your follow-up so that you hit the sweet spot where you have the highest odds of getting a response.

4. Leverage Email Templates:

Question: How can you make it ridiculously easy to send the right follow-up message at the right time every time?

Answer: By lowering the bar for effort and creativity with pre-baked email templates.

Email templates are one of the most powerful weapons in your sales toolbox. If you do nothing else on this list, do this. Start with your most common and repetitive emails and work your way down. The more common the email, the bigger the opportunity to optimize it and yield big results. For example:

- Initial introduction
- In person meeting confirmation
- Post meeting follow up
- Management agreement and related docs
- Etc.

The point here is that you're increasing the bar for quality and consistency of the emails being sent to prospects while simultaneously lowering the bar for effort and creativity enough that agents do not have any excuse not to send out timely, well-written follow-up emails.

Note that the goal here is to ASSIST agents in the sales process, not REPLACE their workload. It is still critical for agents to actively manage their leads and personalize these emails so they don't come across as canned. Unlike drip emails which can foster an out of sight, out-of-mind attitude, email templates provide convenience while still requiring the salesperson to engage with the prospect and their specific needs.

Why anyone would leave something this important up to chance or want to recreate the same emails from scratch over and over again is beyond me.

Email templates can be one of your most effective tools. Equip yourself and your agents with well-crafted emails that are battle-tested and proven to be effective at moving prospects toward sales.

5. Track ACTUAL Contact Attempts

So, let's say you put a great system in place, then the question becomes - is anybody using it?

Are leads actually being called?

Are any leads going stale?

These are critical questions, but who's got the time to go back and take notes documenting every call and email?

The solution: Passive Tracking

Find a lead management system that offers tracked phone numbers and email addresses that are able to track and record calls and emails routed through them. Here's how passive tracking works:

The original contact information for each lead is preserved, an alternative set of tracked contact info is also generated for each lead. When you make outbound calls and emails this way, the prospect sees them as coming directly from the phone or email address you're contacting them from (although some systems allow you to dictate a custom Caller ID).

This way, all calls, and emails are stored for each prospect and can be reviewed as needed. Having this information is invaluable for managing sales and is a basic prerequisite for observing what's really going on in your sales process.

There's no substitute for real data about sales activities. Automatically tracking calls and emails is incredibly easy, and there's simply no excuse not to track those activities.

6. Always Get Agreement on Next Steps

If someone genuinely wants you to stop contacting them, you should. Period. But you can often avoid getting to that point by establishing a good rapport and clear expectations. If you end each conversation, regardless of how motivated the prospect is, by asking for permission to follow up with them in a certain period of time, you're always going to be operating in the realm of mutual respect and consideration when you follow up.

For example, if you've got a great prospect who won't be ready to rent it for another six months, it only makes sense to end the call with, "Joe, do you mind if I call you back in 4 months to check in and see how things are moving along?".

If they say no, then you know where you stand. If they say yes, you've got an open door and a clear expectation that you will follow up.

By asking for permission to follow up, you lower your odds of being an annoyance and have a solid footing in the future.

7. Use Content to Expand the Range of Potential Touch Points

Unfortunately, no matter how well you do it, there are only so many times that you can ask "are you ready to buy" before it becomes annoying. This is particularly true when multiple other companies are asking the same thing.

Compelling content can open doors because it allows one to maintain contact in a VALUE ADDED way versus a VALUE ASKING way.

Good content is a serious investment, but it's an investment in the bank account of trust with each and every prospect, and the more you invest, the more you will have to withdraw from. It's sad how few companies understand this.

If you were in real estate, for example, your knowledge about your work is virtually encyclopedic when compared to your average prospect. Smart management companies find ways to leverage that knowledge by creating interesting content that educates and establishes credibility.

This could be anything from a well-done brochure to an FAQ featuring a couple of polished testimonials. Even a simple video answering basic questions about property management and your services can be a game-changer when it comes to building trust and a personal connection with prospects.

Ask yourself what are three significant topics or questions that you deal with over and over again? How can you answer those questions in a way that is thorough and interesting?

Stand out by creating significant value for prospects before asking for the sale. The more you give, the more effective your ask.

8. Track Email Opens and Click Throughs

This is one of my favorite sales hacks; I use it almost daily.

Scenario: I've had a good initial conversation with a prospect, and I know I need to follow up. A follow-up reminder is set, but a few days later, I notice the prospect is rereading the emails I sent over, and I immediately follow up only to have the prospect tell me it was the perfect time because they were just thinking about our previous conversation.

How is this possible? Email open and click-through tracking.

There are a couple of services that offer tracking email opens and click-throughs, including Hubspot, ZOHO Salesforce, etc.

This technology works by adding a tracking pixel to outbound emails that can record when the email is viewed in your prospects' inbox. The same technology helps retailers like Gap or Target track open rates for mass email campaigns.

Tracking email opens and click-throughs give you a huge level of additional insight into which prospects are interested and how they're interacting with the emails you've sent them.

9. Use Call Down Lists

Let's say you want to go back and try to touch base with older leads that were qualified but not yet ready to buy yet?

By "batching" this task, it becomes easier to schedule regular follow-up weekly or monthly (read more about the power of batching). The problem is that this task can become unwieldy if you have to fish around for all those numbers and punch each one into the phone.

A call-down list makes it a breeze to view and click to call a group of leads in quick succession. Assign someone on your team to take one hour a week to go top to bottom and follow up with 20 leads using a call-down list.

Bonus points for being able to sort and filter the list by things like last contact, # of calls made etc.

Call-down lists make it incredibly easy to follow up with a large batch of prospects in a short period of time.

CHAPTER 12

SALES AND MARKETING METRICS

Sales, much like sports, has utilized science to develop elite performers. In both fields, trainers adopt two key scientific elements — metrics and method — to drive practitioners into breaking records and setting new milestones in their game.

In sports, much of the science focuses on the athlete: genetics, biomechanics (movement techniques, training regimen), nutrition, and psychology (for mental toughness, behavioral modifications, and positive visualizations). On the other hand, the use of science in sales focuses on two areas: the seller and the buyer.

Like top athletes, sales superstars also adopt a sales methodology to systematize their gameplay.

Proactive sales psychology to prepare for the toughest buyer objections ahead of time by establishing the right mental and emotional state.

But because selling is a two-way interaction, the science behind sales also covers the other party in the engagement: prospects, leads, or customers, depending on the stage in the sales process at which they are being engaged.

How do you know if your new CRM system is working?

If it isn't...

- Sales don't have the information or tools they need to convert marketing leads

- Leads stall at certain parts of the sales cycle, fall through the cracks, or take way too long to close

- Customers don't stick around

- Marketing, sales, and customer support don't share information or insights with each other

- Your customer support team works overtime but can't get through all of the tickets

But without waiting to see if any or all of that happens, how can you tell? The answer to that lies in tracking CRM metrics.

Metrics are numbers that tell you whether something's working the way it should. Your CRM affects teams and goals across your business — so you need to know it's working!

The following are a few ways to use CRM.

- Set measurable goals

- Determine how well you're closing valuable deals with sales metrics

Let's dive into the world of CRM metrics!

Set Measurable Goals

"What gets measured gets managed." (18)

To measure CRM success, you need to set SMART goals:

- Specific
- Measurable
- Achievable
- Relevant
- Timely

Setting measurable goals upfront makes it easier to measure the effectiveness of your CRM later on.

To make goals measurable, you need to assign key performance indicators (KPIs) to each. A key performance indicator is a quantifiable measure a company uses to determine how well it's meeting its goals. KPIs tell you:

1. If your CRM strategy works
2. If you're on track to meet your CRM goals

If your goal is to increase customer retention, you wouldn't measure the number of open sales opportunities. If your goal is to shorten your sales cycle, you wouldn't measure your email list growth rate.

Sales metrics: How well are you closing valuable deals?

What does sales success look like for your business?

Here are five metrics to measure sales team performance and CRM success.

1. Close rate

Your close rate is the number of deals closed compared to the number of leads in the pipeline. If you have 100 leads in your pipeline and only ten closed, your close rate is 10%.

It's the holy grail of sales metrics.

Pretty much every sales team under the sun uses close rate as a measure of success — but close rate alone doesn't always tell the whole story.

What's the missing information?

☒ Business 1 closes 75% of their deals.

☒ Business 2 only closes 5% of their deals… but makes more money. How?

Higher average deal size.

Make sure to look at average deal size alongside close rate. How much are your closed deals actually worth? Compare your close rate for the six months leading up to the implementation of a new CRM system

with the six months after. If your CRM's doing its job, your close rate should increase.

If it decreases, it's time to take a close look at your sales team's productivity and the quality of your leads.

3. Net-new revenue

New revenue means spending from new customers. How long a customer stays "new" depends on your business model.

☒ If you sell yearly subscriptions, new revenue is the revenue generated by customers within their first year.

☒ If you sell one-time products, new revenue is the revenue generated by customers' first purchases.

Why measure net-new revenue? It tells you how much money your sales team is making. Tracking new revenue and close rate tells you how valuable your newest batch of customers is.

What can you do with the right CRM in place?

☒ You should be able to identify more high-value deals

☒ You should be able to close more high-value deals

☒ Your net-new revenue should steadily increase

4. Length of each pipeline stage

How long does the average lead stay in each stage of your pipeline?

Stages are the steps of your pipeline (or sales process). Tracking stages helps you find bottlenecks in your sales process (like if deals tend to get stuck in a certain pipeline stage).

Let's say leads stay in the proposal creation step 10x longer than any other step. Sure, creating proposals takes time, but how can you help your sales team move these leads to the next step more quickly?

- Is there a way to automate some of the proposal creation process?

- Do you have proposal templates?

- If so, are they easy to use (and is your team using them)?

The more effective your CRM system is, the faster deals move through each stage of your pipeline.

5. Length of sales cycle

Also called the lead velocity, it measures how long the average deal takes to close. If a lead's first conversation with your sales team is in early January, and they make a purchase or sign a contract in early July, your sales cycle is about six months long.

These two factors play a big role in the length of
sales cycle:

1. Number of decision makers involved

2. Cost of product or service

The more people involved in the decision to purchase, the longer it will take to close. The same goes for price: the more expensive the product or service, the longer the sales cycle. Those factors are out of your sales team's control. But you want to speed upteam's control. But you want to speed up

the sales process and close deals more quickly.

This is exactly what CRM software was made for.

CRM makes your sales process more efficient, meaning you can sell more in less time. A match made in heaven! Keep an eye on this metric over time as a way to measure CRM success.

HOW TO EXCEL AT PHONE SALES

With smartphones taking over the entire world, it is increasingly becoming an essential aspect for businesses. Here, you will find my best key takeaways and tactics for running successful sales calls, based on my 10+ years of sales experience. As the field moves closer to a customer-centric paradigm, you'll find that most of the tactics I have included are buyer-focused.

15 Expert Phone Sales Tips

1. Start all sales calls with a bang

Always start your sales calls in style. One study tried to figure out how to increase room service tips for waiters in hotels. Much to the researchers' surprise, all the waiters had to do was start with a positive comment. When hotel guests opened their doors, waiters said "good morning" and gave a positive weather forecast for the day.

How does this help you? Never start your sales calls or meetings by talking about bad weather, traffic, or being busy. Always begin with a positive comment or anecdote. Think great weather, fun weekend plans, or a favorite sports team winning a game. That kicks most sales calls off on the right foot.

2. Don't bad-mouth competitors during sales calls

The biggest self-sabotaging mistake during a sales call is to speak ill of a competitor. Due to a psychological quirk called spontaneous trait transference, research has shown that whenever you say bad things about someone else; your audience puts those same traits on you.

If you say your competitor is low quality and unreliable, your potential client can't help but associate those traits with you, even if they know logically that you are talking about a third party. So no matter what, when it comes to gossip about competitors, always say, "There are some good and bad providers out there like any industry."

3. Use awesome labels

Assigning a positive label or trait (like having high intelligence or being a good person) to people generally compels them to live up to the label. In one study about fundraising, the researchers told average donors that they were, in fact, among the highest donors.

Can you guess what happened? Those donors proceeded to donate an above-average amount. We tend to live up to positive labels ascribed to us by people we interact with.

When you are with a client or potential customer, give them good labels. Be sure, though, that the labels are sensible and genuine. Never attempt anything that will push people into thinking that you are inauthentic, fake, or manipulative.

For example, you can say, "You are one of our best customers" or "You're such a pleasure to do business with." Having received the compliment, the client will want to be one of your best customers or try even harder to be a pleasing business partner.

4. Set the agenda and stay in control

When I get on sales calls that I've set up from meeting requests, I always like to articulate clear agendas and ask the prospects if that's okay with them. This way, I can keep calls on track and accomplish what I want to achieve while making customers feel that they are in control of the conversation.

For example, you might say, "Well, I'm glad we're able to connect today. I'd love to go over XYZ and then would be happy to answer any questions you might have. How does that sound to you?"

5. Stand up

Allow your passion and excitement for the product to come through in your sales calls. Make it something the prospect can be infected by. In my experience, sales reps can achieve this by standing up and doing sales calls in a main common space instead of hiding in a cubicle or a conference room.

As Mattermark CEO Danielle Morrill says, "Speak loud and proud!" I personally prefer to pace around while making sales calls.

6. Use emphasis wisely

Highlighting certain words or phrases is an effective communication tool that helps you convey your message better. Focus on your inflection, especially on voicemails. Bedrock Data CEO John Marcus describes this as "putting makeup" on your calls. By adding inflection to the right words, you sound more passionate and articulate and, in turn, more convincing.

7. Simplify options

Too many options can easily confuse buyers, making it harder for them to select, rationalize, and affirm a purchase decision. Unless you are a data analytics engine, information overload rarely delivers a benefit.

When describing your product, reduce the number of options and features you want the prospect to focus on. This way, they can arrive at a decision faster and feel more confident that they are not missing out on anything. Only when the likelihood of attrition/rejection becomes overwhelming should you present countermeasures (i.e., the next tier of options).

8. Adopt smart product positioning

The way you frame your product often spells the difference between a closed deal and a lost opportunity. Groundbreaking research in behavioral economics confirm that framing matters. For example, saving $10 feels oddly different across varied buying scenarios (purchasing a smartphone vs. buying a shirt) even when the amount saved is exactly the same. In many cases, relative positioning beats pricing in making brands more appealing to consumers.

Packaging the product as a solution instead of just a commodity or service also increases the likelihood of conversion. At the end of the day, you perform better by solving problems than by selling products.

9. Get emotional

The key finding of behavioral economics is that people rarely hinge their purchase decisions on solidly rational grounds. In most cases, people buy stuff mainly because of emotional triggers and other hyper-personal, sometimes illogical factors.

Nostalgia, brand loyalty, associative/sentimental attachments to a product, and other intangible benefits can serve as persuasion levers as much as a product's technical features.

When engaging prospects, probe for the emotional button that can sway their purchase decision. Articulate a product's value through the use of relevant and powerful storytelling. In some instances, adopting the pleasure-pain dichotomy may work. People's aversion to pain or their deep anticipation of pleasure can be leveraged as powerful selling tools depending on the situation.

Lastly, personal trust — however misplaced — also works in selling, as social media recommendations prove. People will believe an idea or buy a product if these are endorsed by family, friends, or influencers they trust. As a seller, you can pull this powerful string through referrals, testimonials, and influencer marketing.

10. Clarify the product's value

Make it easier for prospects to assess a product's subjective (emotion-based) and objective (fact-based) benefits. Use storytelling and framing techniques to set your product apart from other options available in the market. Whenever possible, have an ROI calculator/formula at hand to help prospects quantify the benefits of the product when emotional triggers are inadequate to push them towards a firm decision. In either case, clearly demonstrate that the value customers receive more than justifies the price.

11. Empower customers

People enjoy discovering stuff that makes them feel good or solutions that address their pesky problems. But they resent being forced, wrangled, goaded, or tricked into a purchase decision.

Because business is leaning more towards a subscription-based paradigm, brands aim to build long-term relationships with customers. If people perceive that you are force-feeding terms or tricking them into buying, you'll lose not just customers but a revenue stream. Hence, give customers enough space, freedom, and power to make purchase decisions they will not regret. You can achieve this by closely involving customers in developing the solutions they need. Get their feedback and give them a semblance of control in the problem-solving process. But always direct the conversation towards your value proposition

12. There's a time for everything

In life, as in sales, timing matters. Depending on your industry and the specific prospect you are engaging, the proper timing for making calls, doing presentations, sending emails, scheduling meetings, and attempting a close exist. A number of studies pinpoint the specific times within a day best suited for reaching out to your target consumers. Find one for your niche and implement it accordingly.

13. Serve hot not cold

Practically speaking, cold calling is becoming a relic of the past. With business intelligence software, social media, and other digital resources, approaching a prospect without any clue about who they are and what they need has become a grossly desperate if not an outright stupid move to make.

Plan and prepare for each call. Use business intelligence tools, corporate databases, and search engines to profile a company. Probe their social media accounts to discover pain points and other opportunities.

Participate in their conversations and identify the values, thought leaders, and brands they associate with. Know as much as you can about a prospect to make them feel important, that you have done your homework, and care about their success.

14. Observe, record, and predict

Much of science involves carefully observing nature, recording your findings, and making predictions based on your observations. Sales follow a similar framework.

The key is to limit your talk time and listen to what your prospects are saying. When prospects talk extensively about their situation, you have already pulled the right strings. Keep them talking. Observe their behavior. Discern their needs based on their statements. Design and propose a solution that squarely addresses their problems.

Ask the right questions. Probe for relevant answers. And truly listen. That is what top-notch selling is all about.

15. But it's also about you

Selling is a two-way street. Even if you take care of customers but neglect honing your skills and attitude as a sales practitioner, you won't go as high as you could.

Customers warm up to and trust business contacts who are masters at their craft. Train to be the very best at what you do so customers will see that your solutions are peerless and they will lose significant value when they move to another vendor.

Think big and set higher goals to challenge yourself and your team. As behavioral economists suggest, organize your goals into several mini objectives that incrementally increase in difficulty. Perform the easy ones first to establish a string of successes that will give you the momentum, confidence, and motivation you need to beat more challenging goals later on.

Selling is a science

Long considered as the art of persuasion, sales has also become a science-driven profession. Business intelligence, data analytics, behavioral modification, and key performance indicators are just some of the elements that systematize the seller side of the dynamic. On the other hand, neuroscience, consumer psychology, and behavioral economics now pervade how smart practitioners approach the buyer side.

Science clearly has a central role in exponentially improving sales performance. With machine learning and artificial intelligence on the rise, the influence of science in the world of sales can only go deeper. The key for tomorrow's sales professionals is to embrace science-backed selling tactics to transform their gameplay and win.

Some other Useful Phone Sales Tips

Make Sure You're Comfortable on the Phone

There are a few basic characteristics everyone needs in a phone-centric career, like sales. Don't have the characteristics outlined below? Either practice until you do or look for another gig.

Enthusiasm:

Be eager to discuss your client's background, pain points, and goals. Your prospect can sense when you sound bored or uninterested and will be less willing to open up. So, ramp up your enthusiasm until you're both excited to find a solution for their use case.

Patience:

Be ready to listen. Don't rush your prospect through the conversation because you never know when a tangent might lead to valuable insights that will help you close. Be firm in guiding the conversation, but allow enough time for the prospect to share openly.

Passion:

If you don't love what you're talking about, how can you expect anyone else to? Passion is critical to selling. Of course, very few of us are "passionate" about selling software, cars, or service packages, so we have to find an angle that does make us excited. If your software helps users get promoted or frees up time they can spend with their families, that's something to get passionate about. Tell yourself a story that motivates and inspires you, and you'll have the same effect on others.

Confidence:

Be comfortable sharing your views. Everyone -- including prospects -- wants honesty. Tell them if you think a prospect might not be a good fit for your product/service. If you don't have a feature your prospect wants, be honest about it and propose solutions or product roadmaps that prove you're proactively thinking about ways forward. Your confidence sets the tone of the call, so be authoritative and proactive.

Sense of Humor:

Don't take yourself or your sales call too seriously. Have a little fun and help your prospect relax. You might try a trusty joke ("Want to hear a joke about a piece of paper? Never mind... it's tearable.") or self-deprecating humor, but break the ice, and it'll be much easier when you press for the next steps.

Be Prepared:

Never dial the phone without preparing. Whether you're taking your first call or your 400th, there are a few things you should do before every meeting:

Define your purpose: Ask yourself what you want to achieve during this call and how you'll get there. Prepare questions in advance: What questions do you need to ask to achieve your goal?

Brainstorm answers:

What are likely responses your prospect will have to your questions? By thinking these through ahead of time, you'll anticipate push-back and tangential questions and be more --prepared to answer them.

Practice:

Whether pitching a new product or giving the same spiel you've orated a hundred times, check in every few months to see how you're doing. Record yourself giving a practice presentation and conduct your own call review to tune up your demo.

Visualize:

Put up a picture of your caller -- or another person -- and pretend you're talking to them while they're on the phone. Sound creepy? Maybe. Does it help you speak to the disembodied voice at the end of the line like they're a real person? Absolutely.

Dress the part:

Would you be confident if the caller saw you? If not, that'll project over the phone. Dress in a way that makes you feel great, and your caller will pick up on it.

Achieve a Relaxed Voice:

You can sense when someone's smiling on the phone, right? It's not just your imagination. Talking with a grin creates a higher frequency in your mouth, which changes the tone of your voice and reassures the listener. To practice this technique, record a sentence in your own non-smiling style. Then record the same words again with a smile and notice the difference. Also, you can achieve a relaxed and persuasive tone by putting your voice's most powerful tools to work. Here's how:

Pace:

Speak too slowly, and your listener might get bored or frustrated. Speak too fast, and they may mishear. An expert caller will mirror the pace of the person they're speaking with. And remember: It takes 10-30 seconds to adjust to a new voice, so give your listener time to adjust to you before diving into the most important part of your presentation.

Volume:

A drawn-out, high-pitched voice says, "I don't believe what I'm hearing," while a low-and-slow pitch says, "I want to be left alone." Aim for an emphatic, high-pitched volume telling your listener you're enthusiastic. And, of course, avoid sounding loud and abrupt because that says you're angry and not open to discussion.

Tone:

Don't apologize for "interrupting" with your call. This sounds like you've done something wrong -- which you haven't. Instead, act as if this call is doing your listener a favor.

Clarity:

Be clear and concise in what you stress in your presentation. Consider the meaning of a sentence and how important the stress of each word can be. Take these examples:

Apathetic: "What would you like us to do about it?"

Defensive: "What would you like me to do about it?"

Curious: "What would you like me to do about it?"

Convince Your Listener:

The key to running professional calls is being aware of how your physical cues are impacting your prospect and the energy of your meeting. Here are a few things to be aware of:

Body language:

It's natural to use your hands as you talk, and that's a good thing. The more you gesture, the more vocal range you use. And when you increase your vocal range, your calls sound natural and conversational. Only 7% of a message is transferred using words. 38% is transferred by the way those words are spoken, and 55% is transferred by body language. Headsets are a great way to free up your hands and let them do the talking during your call.

Non-verbal communication:

Non-verbal sounds, including laughter, sighs, and gasps, are all ways to influence and encourage your listener. Likewise, pausing on and stressing certain words can affect your listener's reception, as we mentioned above.

Good posture:

Yes, really. Your body's posture is important to how you sound on the phone. To achieve the most accurate sound, position the receiver mouthpiece an inch away from your mouth. And remember, your lungs can't fill properly when you're slumped in a chair, which negatively affects your tone and volume. So, sit up straight, and make your mom proud.

Never put them on hold: It's impolite to put your prospect -- or anyone -- on hold without warning or explanation. It also breaks your rhythm and interrupts the connection you've built with your prospect. If something urgent does come up and you have to interrupt your call, never place someone on hold for more than 20-30 seconds without offering to reschedule the meeting.

Use Your Call Script Successfully

Call scripts are there for a reason. Practice with them, but keep a few other things in mind before you jump on a call:

Quit clichés:

Common sales phrases like "game-changer," "par for the course," and "win-win" are contrived and will turn your caller off. Speak with the conversational, everyday language you'd use with a colleague or even a friend, and try to make your prospect forget they're on a sales call.

Edit:

If you're given a script, edit it to suit your natural vocabulary and way of talking.

Don't read it verbatim:

Many salespeople have scripts but don't read from them directly. Use it as a guide, and you'll sound much more natural.

Have a contingency plan:

If a prospect is busy or you're reaching out for the first time, be prepared for them to try fleeing the phone as quickly as possible. When this happens, break from your script and pull out your contingency plan. For example, if a prospect says, "I'm actually in the middle of something right now," try responding, "That's totally fair. Would you mind if I take 30 seconds just to tell you why I called? If it doesn't make sense, you can hang up. Does that sound OK?" You're more likely to catch your prospect off guard and keep them on the phone.

Be a Good Listener:

Easier said than done. Many salespeople railroad their prospects with too many questions, giving them little or no time to respond.

Others ask too few questions and simply throw out solutions without really understanding their prospect's unique use case. Here are a few tips for being a good listener who really "gets" your prospect:

Don't interrupt:

When face-to-face, we give non-verbal cues like shifting slightly, opening our mouths, and nodding to let the other person know we have something to add. Over the phone, those non-verbal cues aren't available. But that doesn't mean you should interrupt. Hold your thoughts until there's a natural break in the conversation to avoid sounding impatient or rude.

Show you're listening:

Try reflective listening by adding an occasional "yes," "hmm," and "I see" as you listen. Make sure these phrases don't overpower the speaker. Instead, pepper them into the conversation to let your prospect know you're on the same page.

Avoid background noise: Show your caller they have your full attention by avoiding background sounds like typing, rustling, or radio/television. If you work on a busy sales floor, book a conference room so you and your prospect aren't distracted by background activity.

Have Great Timing:

The best time to conduct outreach is on Thursdays between 8:00 am and 10:00 am and again between 4:00 pm and 5:00 pm. The worse time to call someone is on Tuesdays between 11:00 am and 2:00 pm.

You can also use timing to get a leg up on your competitors. Know they're calling prospects between 9:00 am and 5:00 pm? Try phoning prospects outside this timeframe to stand out and maybe reach high-level prospects who normally have a gatekeeper screening their calls.

Stay Positive:

Don't overwhelm prospects with your intense enthusiasm. Starting a sales call with an eager "Hey! How are you [prospect name]!?" might come off as pushy and inauthentic.

Maintain a genuine tone and mirror your prospect's demeanor. A less salesy way to keep things light is by sprinkling positive language into your call. Here are a few examples of cheerful language:

"Brilliant,"

"Certainly,"

"You're welcome,"

"Fantastic,"

"It's my pleasure,"

"Of course,"

"Immediately"

"It's no trouble"

"I will find out for you"

"Absolutely"

"Rest assured"

"Wonderful"

"Please"

"Thank you"

"That's great"

And don't forget to establish rapport. The best way to start off on a positive note is to be polite, honest, and personalized with your prospect. Use their name, give them your full attention, and take ownership of follow-up and next steps.

Close with Style:

All of this is worth nothing unless you close the call well. Be clear, offer a review of what you've discussed, and always thank your prospect for their time.

Give verbal signs the call is ending: A common way to do this is by giving a summary of the discussion and offering the next steps.

Make sure you've covered it all: Ask your prospect, "Is there anything we didn't cover that I can speak to before we end the call?"

Always say thank you: Never end a call without thanking your prospect for their time and attention. They didn't have to take your call, so acknowledging their busy schedule is always appreciated.

Successful phone calls are an art. Master these techniques and see more deals move forward, and your peers and managers take notice.

References

1. "American Society for Training and Development (ASTD)". Sales Competency Project. Archived from the original on 2008-09-21. Retrieved 2017-03-07.

2. Putthiwanit, C.; Ho, S.-H. (2011). "Buyer Success and Failure in Bargaining and Its Consequences". Australian Journal of Business and Management Research. 1 (5): 83–92. (from wikipedia)

3. Jason Fernando, Janet Berry Johnson, Article published online, Investopedia, Feb 18 2021. Article link: https://www.investopedia.com/terms/a/accounting.asp

4. American Institute of Certified Public Accountants. CPA Licensure, "https://www.aicpa.org/becomeacpa/licensure.html" Aug. 6, 2020.

5. U.S. Securities and Exchange Commission. "All About Auditors: What Investors Need to Know, web link: https://www.sec.gov/reportspubs/investor-publications/investorpubsaboutauditorshtm.html June 24, 2002

6. Alicia Tuovila, David Kindness, Managerial Accounting, Investopedia, Sept 2020.

7. Transfer Price vs. Standard Cost: What's the Difference?, Investopedia Article, July 28, 2019. Link: https://www.investopedia.com/ask/answers/060915/what-difference-between-transfer-price-and-standard-cost.asp

8. What is a key performance indicator (KPI)? Website link: https://kpi.org/KPI-Basics

9. Csikszentmihalyi, TED talks, Feb 2004.

10. Flow, Mihaly Csikszentmihalyi, 1990. Page no. 74.

11. Sweetening the Till: The use of candy to increase restaurant tipping, Journal of Applied Social Psychology, David B. Strohmetz et al. July 31, 2006

12. "Dr. Robert Cialdini and 6 principles of persuasion" by Tom Polanski: Published online, link: https://jacobmcmillen.com/wp-content/uploads/2017/01/E_Brand_principles.pdf

13. Create a Business vision, Business Queensland, Queensland Government, Australia. Website Link:https://www.business.qld.gov.au/starting-business/planning/business-planning/vision

14. Vision: How leaders develop it, share it, and sustain it, Joseph V. Quigley, Business Horizons, 1994, vol. 37, issue 5, 37–41

15. The Art of Immersion, Frank Rose, 1989.

16. Your Brain on Fiction, The New York Time, Annie Murphy Paul, March 17 2012.

17. 4 Dominant Follow Up strategies, Leadsimple, Web link: https://www.leadsimple.com/sales-course/follow-up-tactics

18. – Peter Drucker, The Price of Management (1954)

19. – Steven Levitt, Co-author of Freakonomics

CPSIA information can be obtained
at www.ICGtesting.com
Printed in the USA
BVHW060942151121
621680BV00009B/450